Paul-Louis Courier (1772–1825)

Medieval and Early Modern French Studies

Series Editor
Noël Peacock

Volume 22

PETER LANG
Oxford - Berlin - Bruxelles - Chennai - Lausanne - New York

Paul-Louis Courier (1772–1825)

Dissident Author under Louis XVIII

IAN R. MORRISON

PETER LANG
Oxford - Berlin - Bruxelles - Chennai - Lausanne - New York

Bibliographic information published by the Deutsche Nationalbibliothek. The German National Library lists this publication in the German National Bibliography; detailed bibliographic data is available on the Internet at http://dnb.d-nb.de.

A catalogue record for this book is available from the British Library.

Library of Congress Control Number: 2024031349

Cover design by Peter Lang Group AG

ISSN 1661-8653
ISBN 978-1-80374-523-7 (print)
ISBN 978-1-80374-524-4 (ePDF)
ISBN 978-1-80374-525-1 (ePub)
DOI 10.3726/b21931

Published by Peter Lang Ltd, Oxford, United Kingdom
info@peterlang.com – www.peterlang.com

This publication has been peer reviewed.

In memory of my late wife, Janet Burnett Morrison (1943–2022)

Contents

Acknowledgements

Small parts of this monograph are derived, with modifications, from work which I have previously published. I am grateful to Peter Lang Group AG for permission to reuse material from *Leonardo Sciascia's French Authors* (Bern: Peter Lang, 2009), ch. 2. The material is present mainly in Chapter 2.

Some of Chapter 6 is based on articles published by the Société des amis de Paul-Louis Courier in the *Cahiers Paul-Louis Courier*: '"Ce garçon-là ira loin". Courier et le style', 5/2 (2016), 45–58; and 'Courier et Napoléon Bonaparte', 5/9 (2023), 5–14.

It is a great pleasure to thank my friend Dr Michael Haren, formerly of the Irish Manuscripts Commission and University College Dublin, for advice on the question of sovereignty; and likewise, to thank my friend and former colleague Hugh Dauncey, for support in many matters.

Preface

Paul-Louis Courier was an artillery officer, a landowner, and above all an author whose legacy includes a dialogue, over thirty pamphlets, several translations from ancient Greek, some occasional pieces and over two hundred letters. I shall consider some of his letters from Italy for their critical content, although they were not published in his lifetime. In his day, he was known mainly for political pamphlets, often designed to defend individual freedom against the authorities, and these political texts are our main concern here. According to Michel Crouzet, 'il a agi en politique par la toute-puissance du ridicule' (*Éc*, 33). Though that may overstate Courier's practical impact, his pamphlets impressed sympathetic contemporaries such as Stendhal and Béranger, and so disturbed the authorities that he was prosecuted twice and imprisoned once. As a writer, he has been widely praised for his style. The historian Bertier de Sauvigny, for example, having associated him with 'la masse des écrivains de second rang qui ont monnayé pour le grand public la doctrine libérale', goes on to distinguish him as being 'l'un des plus grands pamphlétaires de tous les temps; rarement plus de mauvaise foi et plus de bassesse de pensée ont été enveloppées d'un style plus attique, d'une ironie plus cinglante, d'une maîtrise plus grande dans le sous-entendu polisson ou calomnieux'. The great literary scholar Erich Auerbach judged his letters 'von einer leichten und einfachen Vollkommenheit des Stils' but he also noted that, roughly a hundred years after the author's death, he had been 'ziemlich vergessen'.[1] These two verdicts on Courier the writer are the more striking because Bertier and Auerbach disapproved of his outlook. In the English-speaking world, he has attracted no recent scholarly interest. In Italy, he caught the attention of one notable recent author, Leonardo Sciascia, and a selection

1 G. de Bertier de Sauvigny, *La Restauration* (Paris: Flammarion, 1955), 345; Erich Auerbach, 'Paul-Louis Courier', *Deutsche Vierteljahrsschrift für Literaturwissenschaft und Geistesgeschichte*, 4 (1926), 514–47 (pp. 518–19, 515).

of his letters has been translated into Italian.[2] Even in France, despite recent publications such as Crouzet's edition of his pamphlets (2007), and biographies by Jean-Pierre Lautman (2001) or Alain Dejammet (2009), his work still seems neglected. Perhaps he has suffered from the lack of interest in the Bourbon Restoration as a whole. More specifically, his writing had general implications but often sprang from local controversies and, as the events have been forgotten, the point of his interventions has become obscure. His focus on particular cases also means that he expresses his ideas piecemeal, not systematically, which may be why some critics are lukewarm about his thought. Sainte-Beuve, for example, wrote that 'il voit bien, mais par parties, il a de vives idées, mais elles ne sont ni très-variées ni très-abondantes',[3] and later scholars have not challenged this assessment. Amongst the recent studies mentioned above, Lautman's biography often seeks to defend Courier against accusations, for example, that he was a bad soldier or a thief. This work is valuable, especially on questions of local history, but does not examine Courier's literary qualities in detail. Dejammet's biography is more panoramic and attempts, for example, to relate Courier's views to contemporary political thinking. Unusually, Dejammet also pays due attention to the existence of Mme Courier. However, the work is slightly superficial and also suffers from arbitrary segmentation of Courier's life. Crouzet's edition offers a first serious analysis of Courier's authorial characteristics. The Preface depicts him as a Romantic, that is, an anti-Establishment writer in literature and in politics. In examining Courier's writing, Crouzet mentions many features of his manner, but unfortunately he treats them collectively. (He interprets this mass of features as a hostile reaction to the Establishment and its styles.) Methodologically, the defect of this analysis is that it does not relate stylistic features to particular pamphlets, and thus masks the crucial links between manner and content in individual cases. It may be added, incidentally, that Crouzet's commendable enthusiasm sometimes leads him to write in an effusive manner which readers unfamiliar with Courier may struggle to understand.

2 Ian R. Morrison, *Leonardo Sciascia's French Authors* (Bern: Peter Lang, 2009), ch. 2; Paul-Louis Courier, *Lettere di un polemista*, edited and translated by Antonio Motta (Palermo: Sellerio, 1997).

3 Charles-Augustin Sainte-Beuve, *Causeries du lundi*, 3rd edn, 15 vols (Paris: Garnier, 1858–72), vol. 6, pp. 322–3.

The present study, then, explores Courier's letters, where relevant, and his political pamphlets, with occasional references to other texts. The range of issues over which he adopted a critical stance should emerge clearly and justify application to him of the term 'dissident'. I shall focus both on his ideas about political and social questions, and on his practice as a controversialist defending his own views. More particularly, I shall try to show that his thinking is closely connected with various practical realities, and not simply derived from the commonplaces of French liberalism, as is suggested, for example, by Bertier (above). Thus, he was concerned with French conduct of war, which he had seen as an officer; he was also interested in the treatment of the lower ranks under the Restoration. Above all, as a landowner himself, he knew and wrote about the lives of smallholders and their difficulties: for example, oppressive security legislation, possible challenges to their ownership of land, fiscal pressure, or clerical interference in their activities. As I proceed, I shall consider his qualities as a writer in particular pamphlets and attempt to show amongst other things that, as a controversialist, his expression is multifarious and cannot be reduced to one single style. I shall, however, end by reviewing two general characteristics of his writing which pertain to most of his works, his alleged simplicity and his uses of irony. For the reader's convenience, I begin with a brief overview of Courier's career and main ideas. The subsequent chapters examine his output: first, some letters from his time in the French army in Italy which concern the military and political situation, and then his political pamphlets in roughly chronological order.

Editions and References

As Courier's texts are not all readily available, I cite wherever possible two editions: for his pamphlets, the *Œuvres complètes* (ed. Michel Allem) and *Une Écriture du défi* (ed. Michel Crouzet); for his letters, the *Correspondance générale*, with references to equivalent texts, if any, in the *Œuvres complètes.*

Editions are designated as follows:

CG	*Correspondance générale*, ed. Geneviève Viollet-le-Duc
Éc	*Une Écriture du défi*, ed. Michel Crouzet
OC	*Œuvres complètes*, ed. Michel Allem

Letters in the *Correspondance générale* are identified by letter number, date, volume, and page. For example, Letter 132 appears as 132 [37], April 1806, *CG* I, 223. The number in square brackets is that of the letter as published in the *Œuvres complètes.*

Titles of some works may be abbreviated as follows:

Acad	*Lettre à MM. de l'Académie des Inscriptions et Belles-Lettres*
Âmes	*Aux âmes dévotes de la paroisse de Véretz*
Avertlib	*Avertissement du libraire*
AvertRen	*Avertissement sur la lettre à M. Renouard*
Buffon	*Éloge de Buffon*
Chambres	*Pétition aux deux Chambres*
Conseils	*Conseils à un colonel*
Discours	*Simple Discours*
Gazette	*Gazette du village*
LCens	*Lettres au rédacteur du 'Censeur'*
Livret	*Livret de Paul-Louis, vigneron*
Lpart (1)	*Première Lettre particulière*
Lpart (2)	*Deuxième Lettre particulière*
LRen	*Lettre à M. Renouard*
Pamphlet	*Pamphlet des pamphlets*
Pièce	*Pièce diplomatique extraite des journaux anglais*

Procès	*Procès de Paul-Louis Courier*
Rép (1)	*Première Réponse aux anonymes*
Rép (2)	*Deuxième Réponse aux anonymes*
Villageois	*Pétition pour des villageois que l'on empêche de danser*

Chronology of Courier's Main Writings

1799	*Éloge de Buffon*
1802	*Éloge d'Hélène*
1803 (?)	*Conseils à un colonel*
1810	*Lettre à M. Renouard*
1810–21	*Daphnis et Chloé (translation)*
1816	*Pétition aux deux Chambres*
1819	*Lettre à MM. de l'Académie des Inscriptions et Belles-Lettres*
1819–20	*Lettres au rédacteur du 'Censeur'*
1820	*Lettres particulières*
1821	*Simple Discours, Aux âmes dévotes de la paroisse de Véretz, Procès de Paul-Louis Courier, Avertissement sur la lettre à M. Renouard*
1822–4	*Lettres et articles publiés dans différents journaux [Le Courrier français, Le Constitutionnel, Le Journal du commerce]*
1822	*Pétition pour des villageois que l'on empêche de danser, Réponse aux anonymes (1)*
1823	*Réponse aux anonymes (2), Gazette du village, Pièce diplomatique extraite des journaux anglais, Avertissement du libraire*
1824	*Pamphlet des pamphlets*

Introduction

Courier's Life

Paul-Louis Courier was born on 4 January 1772 in Paris. As officially registered, his parents were Jean-Paul Courier and Louise-Élisabeth Laborde. Jean-Paul had acquired land and forests including the noble estate of Méré in Touraine in 1767. He thus became legally a nobleman, the 'seigneur de Méré'. Though neither he nor Paul-Louis valued this status, it explains why our author is sometimes called Courier de Méré or described as noble. For a time, Jean-Paul also managed the duc d'Olonne's estates and may have had an affair with his wife. Some speculate that she, not Louise-Élisabeth Laborde, was Paul-Louis's mother, since Jean-Paul and Louise-Élisabeth did not marry formally until 1777. But if Paul-Louis had any doubts over the identity of his natural mother, they seem not to have harmed his relations with Louise-Élisabeth, for his letters to her are warm. After his early years in Touraine, in 1784 he moved with his parents to Paris, where he could study mathematics to the standard required for a military career, and where he also studied Greek and Latin.[1] In October 1792, he entered the École d'artillerie in Châlons and qualified as a lieutenant in June 1793. After serving in France, he was posted in 1798 to Rome and repatriated in 1799 when the French garrison capitulated to the Austrians. In 1804 he was sent again to Italy, was involved in a campaign against Calabrian guerrillas (1805–6), and stayed in Italy until he resigned his commission in 1809. After resigning, he changed his mind, sought reinstatement, and reported for duty at Wagram. But there he again decided to resign and left without permission. Though his reinstatement was still awaiting official approval, the army might now have

1 Jean-Pierre Lautman, *Paul-Louis Courier, ou la plume indomptée* (Chambray-lès-Tours: Éditions CLD, 2001), 28, 42–3.

treated him as a serving officer, and court-martialled him for desertion; the risk did not materialize, but the episode probably contributed to his later poor reputation as a soldier.[2] He returned to Italy later in 1809 and remained until 1812.

Initially, his literary interest was in translating or adapting ancient Greek texts, and he published an *Éloge d'Hélène* in 1802.[3] After leaving the army, he continued these studies. In 1809, at the Biblioteca Laurenziana in Florence, he began editing a manuscript of *Daphnis et Chloë* which included a passage missing from published editions. After the passage had been copied, he marked the place with a piece of paper, on which there was wet ink, and the rediscovered passage was partly obliterated. Though he explained that he had not noticed the ink, a pamphlet by the librarian of the Laurenziana, Francesco Del Furia, conveyed the suspicion that Courier had defaced the passage deliberately, to prevent others from studying it. The affair provoked controversy amongst scholars and also brought Courier into conflict with the French authorities in Rome. The Préfecture, perhaps fearing that he would offend Italian opinion, forbade him to answer Del Furia's pamphlet but Courier defiantly published a belligerent riposte, the *Lettre à M. Renouard.* Though the Préfet then reacted mildly, his initial veto probably confirmed Courier's view of himself as an outsider and an opponent of the Napoleonic regime.

He returned to France in 1812, and in 1814 married Herminie, the daughter of Étienne Clavier, his friend and fellow classicist. Courier also bought property in Touraine, notably the forest of Larçay and the estate of La Chavonnière. As a proprietor, he made scant profits and had various disputes with neighbours, timber-merchants, and the mayor of Véretz, Debeaune. Up to 1819, however, he continued to study Greek authors, while producing his first political pamphlet, the *Pétition aux deux Chambres* (1816). As we shall see, this piece concerned the oppression of modest villagers, arbitrarily arrested for trivialities or for Bonapartism, of which they were quite innocent. He knew the case, at least by hearsay, as

2 Alain Dejammet, *Paul-Louis Courier* (Paris: Fayard, 2009), 143–50, and Auerbach (520–1) offer cautious assessments of the affair.

3 Dejammet, ch. 3.

witnessed in his letters to Mme Courier. Initially, he tells her of the arrest of one man, who had not stopped for a funeral procession (500 [175], 27 January 1816, *CG* III, 64). Later, he informs her of the number of arrests and the fate of those arrested (507 [180], 7 November 1816, *CG* III, 73). It does appear that, more broadly, such cases gave him some real insight into the vulnerability of the humble. The same conclusion arises from other texts, such as the *Gazette du Village*, which relates various incidents like the imprisonment of Charles Avenet (*OC*, 193; *Éc*, 414). It is true that Courier could have invented these episodes, but that is unlikely, since the *Gazette* was for immediate publication and was set in an area where the inhabitants would have known each other. But Courier also learnt quickly that the peasants, however modest, were not mere innocents, and that in bargaining with them caution was needed: 'il ne faut pas multiplier les conditions d'un marché. D'ailleurs les paysans calculent' (510, 15 November 1816, *CG* III, 80). In short, his view of the peasantry rested on acquaintance with reality, not simply on abstract principles alone. After the *Pétition aux deux Chambres*, there was a pause in his production of political pamphlets until 1819, when he returned to this kind of writing. As we shall see, his other political pamphlets were sometimes inspired by local events, sometimes by more immediately national questions. On 10 April 1825, he was murdered in the Larçay forest – whether for personal or political motives or for both remains unclear.[4]

Courier's Ideas

In the context of the Restoration, Courier's political sympathies are usually classified as 'liberal'. In order to apprehend the sense of 'liberal', though Courier himself was never a député, it is helpful to start from the spectrum of parliamentary forces in 1815. There were three fluid groupings: ultra-royalists ('ultras'), moderates, and independents. Without forming a compact party, each group had its common priorities. The

4 Lautman, 225–40.

ultras supported hereditary, divine-right monarchy, a major role for the Church and generally a return to the *ancien régime*. The moderates, including the so-called 'doctrinaires', favoured constitutional monarchy. Chateaubriand, though not a député, exemplified such thinking for a time.[5] The independents, the main parliamentary opposition, were initially a mixture of republicans, Bonapartists, orleanists and liberals. However, guided by Benjamin Constant, the opposition became predominantly liberal, while also having affinities with the doctrinaires. There came thus to be two parliamentary groups, ultras and liberals with the latter's various associates.[6] Courier shared certain priorities with the liberals, but incorporated them into his own distinctive outlook.

As political terms, 'libéral' dates from 1750, 'libéralisme' from 1818.[7] This sense of 'libéral' was apparently considered novel, even exotic, as Courier used the Spanish form *Liberales* in his *Pièce diplomatique* of 1823 (*OC*, 193; *Éc*, 430). There is no all-encompassing definition of French liberalism, but liberal thinking has some recurrent themes. One is that, by nature, all men are equal; the idea appears, for example, in Constant's *De la perfectibilité de l'espèce humaine*, in his *Mélanges de littérature et de politique*.[8] Natural equality is intimately associated with another great liberal theme, the individual's natural rights to life and freedom: in principle, if all are equal no one may deprive another of those things. Natural equality and natural rights cannot be mere abstractions, however, but must be buttressed with legal equality. Thus, the *Déclaration des droits de l'homme et du citoyen* (1789), which some describe as a 'liberal' document,[9]

5 François-René de Chateaubriand, *De la Monarchie selon la Charte* (Paris: Le Normant, 1816).

6 Surveys in Bertier, 142–5; and Munro Price, *The Perilous Crown* (London: Pan Macmillan, 2008), 91–3. On the *doctrinaires*, Emmanuel de Waresquiel, 'La Restauration libérale: les doctrinaires et l'éloge du centre (1816–1820)', in *Penser la Restauration 1814–1830* (Paris: Tallandier (Texto), 2020), 149–70.

7 *Trésor de la langue française*, s.v. 'libéral', 'libéralisme'.

8 Benjamin Constant, *Écrits politiques*, ed. Marcel Gauchet (Paris: Gallimard (Folio), 1997), 714.

9 Elisabeth G. Sledziewski, 'Fondations du libéralisme français (1760–1848)', *Raison présente*, 108 (1993), 93–109 (p. 98).

provides, for example, that: 'la loi [...] doit être la même pour tous' (Art. 6).[10] Liberals particularly defended the right to private property, and the *Déclaration* numbered it amongst the 'droits naturels et imprescriptibles de l'homme' (Art. 2).[11] Constant, however, thought that, unlike equality and the rights to life and freedom, the right of any man to own property was not natural but was established by society, to ensure stability and peace. In *De l'inviolabilité de la propriété*, he argued that only recognized rights to property could prevent untrammelled conflict and the triumph of force.[12] The approach to property underlines that liberals were not egalitarian: in practice, to defend universal property rights was, amongst other things, to uphold the sectional interests of the wealthy.

Much in the liberal outlook was a radical departure from the *ancien régime*. To justify such discontinuity, liberals stressed that societies evolve, in particular from warrior societies to trading, commercial communities. Liberals contended that, when countries were poor, peoples had to fight each other for resources, and societies were necessarily organized for war, with ruling elites drawn from a warrior class. But as agriculture developed, the need to fight for resources diminished, and it became advantageous to preserve peace and avoid the disorders of war. In this process, the justification for government by a warrior elite, as in *ancien régime* France, disappeared too. In this evolutionary view of things, certain liberals were also convinced that human nature itself could improve.[13] (Though some used the term 'perfectibilité' in this connection, they did not usually mean that mankind could literally become perfect, but simply that man was capable of moral and intellectual progress.) Mme de Staël, who was an outstanding personality in European literature, famously celebrates such progress in *De la littérature*. In this work she examines at length 'l'influence de la religion, des mœurs et des loix sur la littérature et [...] l'influence de la littérature sur la religion, les mœurs et les loix'. At various points, she underscores the

10 Stéphane Rials, ed., *Textes constitutionnels français*, 17th edn (Paris: Presses Universitaires de France (Que sais-je ?), 2002), 4.

11 Rials, 3.

12 Constant, *Principes de politique* in *Écrits politiques*, 441–2.

13 Regarding social evolution, Constant, *De l'esprit de conquête et de l'usurpation* in *Écrits politiques*, ch. 2.

progressive enrichment of men's minds in 'la marche lente, mais continuelle, de l'esprit humain dans la philosophie'. Such progress varies, but never stops, and is ultimately radical:

> En parcourant les révolutions du monde et la succession des siècles, il est une idée dont je ne détourne jamais mon attention; c'est la perfectibilité de l'espèce humaine. Je ne pense pas que ce grand œuvre de la nature morale ait jamais été abandonné; dans les périodes lumineuses, comme dans les siècles de ténèbres, la marche graduelle de l'esprit humain n'a point été interrompue.[14]

The figurative expression 'grand œuvre' is crucial: it implies complete transformation, as it had in earlier ages referred to the alchemists' quest to transmute base metals into gold.[15] Constant's perspective, meanwhile, was perhaps more intellectual, perhaps less optimistic and certainly more political than Mme de Staël's, in that he highlighted reform produced by the evolution of mentalities, such as 'l'abolition de l'esclavage, qui est pour nous une vérité évidente, et qui était le contraire pour Aristote'.[16] Clearly, both authors are convinced that human progress is, though sometimes hesitant, natural and probably inevitable.[17] But in this regard Courier's view of the world was largely divergent: there is no sign that he believed in unstoppable human progress or indeed that he thought mankind perfectible in any sense. His scepticism was no doubt connected to a generally

14 Germaine de Staël, *De la littérature considérée dans ses rapports avec les institutions sociales*, 2 vols (Paris: Maradan, 1799), vol. 1, i, li.

15 *Petit Robert*, s.v. 'œuvre'.

16 Constant, *De la perfectibilité*, 706–10, 719–20. The 'progressive' outlook inspires the subtitle of the liberal *Censeur européen ou Examen de diverses questions de droit public, et de divers ouvrages littéraires et scientifiques, considérés dans leurs rapports avec les progrès de la civilisation*. For broader surveys of liberal thinking, see Sledziewski, 'Fondations du libéralisme', and Irene Collins, *Liberalism in Nineteenth-Century Europe* (London: The Historical Association, 1957). Collins highlights the tension between liberal ideas about perfectibility and Catholic teaching on original sin (pp. 15–16).

17 On Constant and progress, see, however, Biancamaria Fontana, *Benjamin Constant and the Post-Revolutionary Mind* (New Haven: Yale University Press, 1990), especially chapter 3. Fontana concludes that Constant's opinions varied, and that for him, progress was a powerful aspiration rather than a certainty.

low estimate of human nature. Writing to a lady in Paris, he proclaims both his devotion to her and also the desirability of another Flood:

> Il ne faut point trop détester le genre humain quoique détestable; mais si l'on pouvait faire une arche pour quelques personnes comme vous Madame, et noyer encore une fois tout le reste, ce serait une bonne opération. Je resterais sûrement dehors; mais vous me tendriez la main [...] sachant que je suis et serai toute ma vie, Madame ... (132 [37] April 1806, *CG* I, 226)

Though this is a light-hearted compliment to the recipient, the suggestion that almost all of mankind deserves to be drowned is symptomatic. Nevertheless, Courier did envisage two sorts of progress. He was mainly interested in the legal and social progress of the humble. Much less prominently, he also treated intellectual progress as a reality, but in his writing, as we shall see, he used the idea to criticize reactionary courtiers (*LCens* IX), and backward attitudes in the Roman Catholic Church (*Rép*. (2)).

A first feature of Courier's own thinking is his attention to the fate of the common people. Lautman notes 'la haute idée qu'il se faisait du peuple', unlike most liberals, who 'parlaient [...] des hautes classes et ne réclamaient la liberté que pour elles'. Likewise, the historian Michel Winock calls Courier and the songwriter Béranger 'libéraux du peuple'.[18] To use Lautman's themes, we may ask what Courier understood by 'peuple' and by 'liberté'. Regarding the first, he shows limited interest in city-dwellers, and only the *Livret de Paul-Louis, vigneron* (1823) refers much to them. In practice, his 'peuple' is the peasantry, with which he identifies in his first *Réponse aux anonymes* (1822): 'je serai du parti du peuple, des paysans comme moi' (*OC*, 154; *Éc*, 383). As France's population was 80–85% rural,[19] this focus may seem inclusive, but his concerns are quite selective, for he rarely mentions tenant farmers or agricultural labourers, and concentrates on smallholders. Typically, the *Simple Discours* (1821) lauds Henri IV, 'le roi du peuple [...] protecteur déclaré de la petite propriété' (*OC*, 74; *Éc*, 263). Courier's emphasis on smallholding is unusual amongst liberals, who were

18 Lautman, 189; Michel Winock, *Les Voix de la Liberté: les écrivains engagés du XIXe siècle* (Paris: Éditions du Seuil, 2001), 76.

19 Jean Tulard, *Les Français sous Napoléon* (Paris: Hachette, 1978), 13; Bertier, 236–8. On urban workers, Tulard, *Les Français sous Napoléon*, 225–40; Bertier, 250–7.

mostly concerned with larger estates and indeed with wealth of all kinds. Constant, for example, praised the socially stabilizing role of old money and of wealth honestly earned: 'les anciens propriétaires sont les appuis naturels d'un monarque légitime'; and 'dans une société bien organisée, le talent conduit à la richesse'.[20] While smallholders were Courier's main concern, he also showed some interest in the lower ranks of the army. Certainly, he thought that smallholders and ordinary soldiers were the groups that would suffer most if the old order returned, bringing 'pour le peuple, des impôts; pour les soldats [...] du pain noir et des coups de bâton' (*Livret*, *OC*, 174; *Éc*, 398). His concern with the 'peuple' was complemented by dislike of those who seemingly enjoyed a parasitical existence: the royal court, the king's ministers, the Church, and the nobility. Typically, the *Pétition pour des villageois que l'on empêche de danser* records that the working population's taxes support 'mendiants, moines, laquais, courtisans' (*OC*, 137; *Éc*, 345). Courier satirizes different parasites in different contexts, but always assumes this active/inactive dichotomy. While his interest in the 'peuple' is unusual, his overall vision of a society divided between producers and parasites is shared by various liberal thinkers. Charles Comte wrote, for example: 'il n'existe dans le monde que deux grands partis; celui des hommes qui veulent vivre des produits de leur travail ou de leurs propriétés, et celui des hommes qui veulent vivre sur le travail ou sur les propriétés d'autrui'.[21]

Courier's defence of 'liberté', goes naturally enough with his focus on the 'peuple', for it often involved defending the poor. However, he recognized that the oppressed could belong to any social group. His second *Lettre particulière* describes a meeting of electors in November 1820, where he overhears a neighbour advising others to vote for Courier himself: 'il n'aime pas Bonaparte, mais il ne veut point qu'on emprisonne les bonapartistes [...] Aristocrate sous Robespierre, libéral en 1815, il va être pour vous, et ne vous renoncera que quand vous serez forts' (*OC*, 64; *Éc*, 245). In reporting this advice, whether real or invented, Courier conveys that he supports

20 *De l'esprit de conquête et de l'usurpation* in *Écrits politiques*, 192–3.

21 'De la multiplication des pauvres, des gens à places et des gens à pensions', *Censeur européen*, 7 (1818), 1–2; Mark Weinburg, 'The Social Analysis of Three Early Nineteenth-Century French Liberals: Say, Comte, and Dunoyer', *Journal of Liberal Studies*, 2 (1978), 45–63 (p. 53).

the downtrodden, irrespective of their politics or social position. As the oppressed were usually poor, the passage casts no doubt on his concern with the 'peuple', but it does mean that, in this respect at least, his interest in the humble was not exclusive.

What did Courier mean by 'liberté'? He rarely discusses individual freedom in general, abstract terms, and suggests indeed that his own attachment to it is rather temperamental than philosophical: 'j'aime la liberté par instinct, par nature' (*Rép.* (1), *OC*, 148; *Éc*, 377). However, when the agronomist Jacques Bujault urges the government to do more to encourage agriculture, Courier replies: 'Laissez le gouvernement percevoir des impôts et répandre des grâces; mais, pour Dieu, ne l'engagez point à se mêler de nos affaires' (*LCens* II, 12; *Éc*, 184). Reference to 'nos affaires' implies that there are public and private spheres, of which the former, but not the latter, concerns the state. Courier does not specify where the boundary lies, save to say that collecting and spending taxes are the state's business, but locating individual freedom outside the public sphere was probably a notion familiar enough to liberals. In his lecture *De la liberté des anciens comparée à celle des modernes* (1819), Constant notes that, as the populations of ancient city-states were small, they could be governed by assemblies of citizens, and men's freedom then lay in their participation in making laws and other political decisions. It resided in what Constant saw as the public sphere. But in 1819 states were too populous for such arrangements, and freedom must be enjoyed in a private sphere. For Constant, 'Le but des modernes est la sécurité dans les jouissances privées; et ils nomment liberté les garanties accordées par les institutions à ces jouissances'.[22] Freedom has become essentially freedom from arbitrary use of power: 'pour chacun le droit de n'être soumis qu'aux lois, de ne pouvoir ni être arrêté, ni détenu, ni mis à mort, ni maltraité d'aucune manière, par l'effet de la volonté arbitraire d'un ou de plusieurs individus'.[23] For the eminent political theorist John Rawls, Constant's is a classic statement of one current of Liberal thinking about individual freedom. According to Rawls, the alternative Liberal tradition,

22 *Écrits politiques*, 602–3.
23 *Écrits politiques*, 593.

derived from Rousseau, emphasizes the individual's involvement in the making of collective decisions[24].

Rather than discuss freedom in general, Courier concentrated on particular freedoms and rights, such as free speech or freedom from arbitrary arrest. Here, he used Louis XVIII's *Charte Constitutionnelle* (1814), to which I now turn. A fundamental question concerned sovereignty, the source of political authority. The Revolution had attributed sovereignty to the people, for example, in the Constitution of 1793 (Arts 25 and 28).[25] In the Preamble to his *Charte*, Louis, on the contrary, styles himself 'Louis, par la grâce de Dieu, roi de France et de Navarre'. Like his forebears, he believed that sovereignty was vested in the Crown by the will of God, and that the people had no part in it. He goes on, stressing his unique authority:

> nous avons volontairement, et par le libre exercice de notre autorité royale, accordé et accordons, fait concession et octroi à nos sujets, tant pour nous que pour nos successeurs, et à toujours, de la charte constitutionnelle qui suit.[26]

Courier probably believed in popular sovereignty, as witness the *Éloge d'Hélène*, which praises Theseus for basing his laws on 'la souveraineté du peuple' (*OC*, 292). The *Éloge* is a slight work, loosely translated from Isocrates's *Encomium of Helen*; however, sovereignty is mentioned where the original offers no obvious counterpart, and Courier's interpolation suggests that he thought the point important. But whereas for some political thinkers, such as Chateaubriand, sovereignty was a fundamental question of principle, it interested Courier rather for its practical implications. If the Crown claimed to grant a constitution by sovereign authority, could it not invoke the same authority to change or withdraw the constitution? For Courier, the very term 'octroi' implied that the *Charte* had been granted as a favour by a superior power which remained superior. The *Pamphlet des pamphlets* (1824) underlines such connotations of 'octroyer' with reference to debates in Britain's American colonies before the War of Independence. Some critics of British rule demanded

24 John Rawls, *Political Liberalism* (New York: Columbia University Press, 1996), 5.

25 Rials, 18.

26 Rials, 48–9.

independence, others would have accepted 'une charte octroyée, dût-elle être bientôt modifiée, suspendue' (*OC*, 216; *Éc*, 457). Implicitly, Courier doubted whether the *Charte* had really been granted 'à toujours', by a king whom he distrusted, as appears in the *Pièce diplomatique* of 1823.

While Louis's conception of sovereignty is retrograde, the *Charte* is progressive in important particulars: Article 1, for example, guarantees legal equality.[27] True, ministers could use extraordinary legislation, *lois d'exception*, to suspend various articles and, though such *lois* needed approval by the legislature, this last safeguard was not always effective. In practice, Courier rarely mentions Article 1 but was keenly interested in several other Articles, especially 4, 8, and 9. Article 4, against arbitrary arrest, declares that a Frenchman's 'liberté individuelle est [...] garantie, personne ne pouvant être ni poursuivi ni arrêté que dans les cas prévus par la loi et dans la forme qu'elle prescrit'. But Article 4 was suspended by a *loi de sûreté générale* (29 October 1815) which enabled the authorities to detain without trial anyone suspected of plotting against the royal family or the security of the State, and the *loi* did not lapse fully until January 1818.[28] Moreover, it seems that the authorities sometimes ignored Article 4, as summary arrests apparently continued after the *loi de sûreté générale* expired. In 1819 Courier claims that a prosecutor could have anyone imprisoned indefinitely with a two-line order stating no grounds: 'gendarmes de courir, prison de s'ouvrir; quand vous y serez, la Charte ne vous en tirera pas' (*LCens IV*, *OC*, 16; *Éc*, 188). Article 8, on free speech, provides that 'les Français ont le droit de publier et de faire imprimer leurs opinions, en se conformant aux lois qui doivent réprimer les abus de cette liberté'. But this freedom too was curtailed drastically: the *loi sur les discours et écrits séditieux* (9 November 1815) forbad anything conveying disrespect for the king, even waving a tricolour.[29] Worse still, Courier's personal experience led him to claim that Article 8 was a trap to incite publication of criticism, and so make it easier to identify and oppress critics (*Rép* (1), *OC*, 151; *Éc*, 380). Article 9, which protected all individuals' rights to own property,

27 Rials, 49.

28 Charles-Antoine Lepec et al. (eds), *Recueil général des lois, décrets, ordonnances etc.* (Paris: Journal des notaires et des avocats, 1839), vol. 14, p. 140.

29 Bertier, 132–3.

explicitly mentioned owners of *biens nationaux*, that is, estates or parts of estates, confiscated by the Revolution from the nobility or the Church, and sold on in small lots to often modest buyers.[30] At the Restoration, the *biens nationaux* became a pressing political issue: the pre-Revolutionary owners now demanded their estates back and Courier doubted whether Article 9 would be upheld against them (e.g. *Discours*, *OC*, 86; *Éc*, 274). Overall, then, his misgivings concerned the permanence and the letter of the *Charte*, and also the spirit in which it was applied. Yet he readily invoked the document because, when he discussed freedom and rights, it was usually to deplore particular authoritarian acts which flouted at least the letter of the *Charte*. The point which must be underlined is that, for him, freedom was a matter of particulars, and his approach was rather legal than philosophical. The *Charte* provided a convenient authority on which to base his arguments.

Another important aspect of relations between government and subjects was taxation, which Courier mentions quite often, but rarely in much detail. For these purposes, a distinction must be made between direct and indirect taxes. The former fell largely on owners of land or other real property, while the latter affected almost everyone: most notorious amongst indirect taxes were the *droits réunis*, a multiplicity of duties levied on almost every stage of the wine trade from production to consumption, but also on other products such as salt and tobacco. The *Charte* stipulates that taxes can be levied only with parliamentary approval:

> ART. 48 Aucun impôt ne peut être établi ni perçu, s'il n'a été consenti par les deux Chambres et sanctionné par le roi.
>
> ART. 49 L'impôt foncier n'est consenti que pour un an. Les impositions indirectes peuvent l'être pour plusieurs années.[31]

Here, 'impôt foncier' is direct taxation, and the obligation to have it approved annually implies that it was a more sensitive matter than indirect taxes. It was more sensitive because it immediately affected députés and

30 Tulard, *Les Français sous Napoléon*, 20–2; Thierry Lentz, *Napoléon: Dictionnaire historique* (Paris: Perrin, 2020), 333–5.

31 Rials, 53.

voters, who were all men paying direct taxes above certain thresholds. A narrow category of taxpayers could thus be said to consent, through their députés, to the taxes, direct or indirect, which they had to pay. But this could be said of no one else, and lack of consent is clearly a problem of principle. However, neither this point nor indeed taxation as such seem to have greatly concerned liberal thinkers. In general, they accepted taxation as a necessary evil and urged simply that it be minimized to avoid detriment to economic activity. Courier was more recalcitrant, as we shall see, particularly in the *Gazette du village*.

A last facet of Courier's outlook is less political than social, namely his attention to prescriptive moral rules. He obviously mentions such matters as theft and licentiousness in criticizing corrupt ministers and courtiers. But he is also attentive, for practical reasons, to the day-to-day morals of the 'peuple'. As he stresses in the *Simple Discours* (e.g. *OC*, 82–3; *Éc*, 271), sexual morality favours the orderly family life without which the humble cannot survive. This view is unremarkable, but he also held, rather more distinctively, that morality can exist without religion or priests. The *ancien régime* had relied on the priests to teach morality. The Revolution, often hostile to Catholicism or the clergy or both, sought ways to promote morality without religion.[32] Courier's approach to the matter is thus not unique, but it lends itself to memorable assaults on the depravity of individual churchmen and the perverse effect of institutions such as celibacy of priests, for example, in the second *Réponse aux Anonymes*. In contesting the priests' role as moral teachers, Courier was once again rejecting an invasion by the authorities of private and family life; he was returning to the political theme of freedom. The continuity in his concerns is the plainer because the secular authorities actively supported much clerical intervention in ordinary life, as shown in the *Pétition pour des villageois que l'on empêche de danser*.

Those, then, are some major threads in Courier's thinking about political and social questions. They will reappear frequently in the chapters

32 For instance, Antoine Destutt de Tracy, *Quels sont les moyens de fonder la morale chez un peuple?* (Paris: Agasse, an VI, 1797–8), 26. Courier's own religious beliefs and moral rules are considered in Chapter 4.

that follow. It must also be reiterated that Courier's thinking will be treated here as being of interest in itself. The reader will often find, in the following pages, comparisons between Courier and others, in the liberal political family, particularly Constant. The point of these comparisons is to highlight affinities and divergences; it is not simply to examine the extent to which Courier can be classified as a liberal. Courier is Courier and, as I hope to show, deserves attention in his own right.

CHAPTER I

Letters: Italy, Scholarship, and War

Courier's letters were originally intended to be personal or for communication with other soldiers. It is sometimes assumed that an author's private correspondence will reveal his feelings and opinions more reliably than works meant for publication. Thus Sainte-Beuve attributed particular 'autorité biographique' to Courier's 'lettres toutes naïves, écrites au courant de la plume'.[1] But caution is needed, because editors have sometimes modified the texts. Most such changes were made by Auguste Sautelet, who first published Courier's letters in 1828, and adopted by Allem in the *Œuvres complètes*. Mme Viollet-le-Duc, who used the Courier family archives for her *Correspondance générale*, restores Courier's version, and also records Sautelet's changes. Thus, it is clear that Sautelet omitted some banalities: for example, when Courier discusses lice, toothpicks, or clothes (21 [5], *CG* I, 77–8), they vanish in Sautelet's version (*OC*, 650–1). Vulgarities also disappear, as when Courier wrote to a comrade: 'Supposons que vous fussiez sur le point de faire un bon mariage, irais-je conter au beau-père que vous avez la chaude-pisse?' (169 [57], March 1807, *CG* I, 293). Here, Sautelet offers: 'irais-je conter au beau-père vos fredaines galantes?' (*OC*, 741). Some changes concern graver matters, such as a massacre involving French troops in the village of Cassano allo Ionio. Courier writes that he arrived 'une demi-heure' after events began (147 [49], 1806, *CG* I, 265). But Sautelet has him arrive 'trois jours après' (*OC*, 728). Editorial

1 *Causeries du lundi*, vol. 6, p. 324.

changes by Sautelet and his direct followers thus produce a slightly unreliable picture of Courier.[2]

The author's own revisions are also problematic. By 1825 he planned to publish some of his letters and accordingly had started revising them. Sautelet does not mark Courier's amendments, but Mme Viollet-Leduc's edition indicates most of them. As she shows, Courier transformed some letters and, in an extreme case such as Letter 146 [48] (*CG* I, 255–64), he even wrote several new drafts.[3] Though Courier did not live to publish them, the heavily revised missives are, in principle, akin to any other work intended for publication: they are not necessarily more revealing than writings, such as his pamphlets, written from the outset for publication. With those provisos, we shall examine the relevant correspondence here, particularly for Courier's views on the army and war (including Bonaparte as a military leader). His views are often very critical, but they remained private. This is a point of some importance, because of his later claims to have spoken out against Bonaparte while he was in power.

Courier's own service, from 1793 to 1809, was long for one who later strove to defend his personal freedom and whose chief interest at the time was in classics. One reason for remaining in the army was financial. He had inherited property from his father in 1796 but, after years of absence, he was unsure what the estate was worth and, as he explains to M. d'Agincourt, he could not lightly abandon his pay (234 [92], 15 October 1808, *CG* II, 51). Writing to M. and Mme Thomassin after leaving the army, he seems perhaps regretful of his long service, and certainly delighted by his freedom: 'Quoique dans le vilain métier que j'ai fait si longtemps, je fusse bien moins esclave qu'un autre, je ne connaissais point du tout la liberté' (288 [113], 12 October 1809, *CG* II, 125). His obligations were not always onerous, for he spent long periods away from his unit: sometimes on sick leave, as in 1800–1, sometimes travelling slowly between postings, as from southern Italy to Verona in 1807–8. Long absences were not unusual for

2 Sautelet complemented the letters with some notes about Courier's activity, which are reproduced by Allem, but not Mme Viollet-le-Duc. On the sources of the notes, see *OC*, xvii–xviii; Dejammet, 19, 108.

3 Introduction, *CG* I, 8–9.

officers: Bonaparte, for example, spent some 32 months on leave between November 1785 and February 1791.[4] Even when on duty, Courier often had ample free time, as in Albi or Toulouse (late 1795–late 1797), and in Rome in early 1799. Since he could use his leisure to study, he may well have been 'moins esclave qu'un autre'.

An incidental benefit of soldiering was that it gave him specialist insights into some Greek authors. For example, he tells Mgr Marini that, in editing Xenophon, 'je crois avoir fait tout ce que pouvait faire un soldat, expliquant aux savants ce qu'ils ne peuvent savoir, suivant la loi: *tractant fabrilia fabri* [each man to his own trade]' (201 [79], 6 March 1808, *CG* II, 13). Service in Italy had particular advantages for he could enjoy the country's wealth of natural beauty and relics from antiquity. The twofold appeal of beauty and antiquity is celebrated rather obliquely in a letter to Klewanski (136 [40], 10 June 1806, *CG* I, 232) and mentioned in several others (e.g. 101 [26], 27 February 1805, *CG* I, 178; 173 [61], 25 May 1807 *CG* I, 299). In the last, he writes to Mme Arnoult: 'l'antique! la nature! voilà ce qui me charme, moi; voilà mes deux passions de tout temps'. Along with these fruits of his travels, he mentions the Italian language in letter 136 to Klewanski: 'aurai-je perdu mon temps en apprenant un idiome composé des plus beaux sons que j'aie jamais entendu articuler'. It is believable that these scholarly and aesthetic interests helped keep him in the army, the more so because southern Italy was dangerous. As he told Klewanski, highway robbery was prevalent, and only under arms was it relatively safe to travel (*CG* I, 231–2). He claims, for example, that in the Kingdom of Naples 'une voiture ne peut se hasarder en campagne sans une escorte de 50 hommes armés, qui souvent dévalisent eux-mêmes ceux qu'ils accompagnent' (107 [29], 23 April 1805, *CG* I, 186). Similar remarks, mainly about Apulia, appear in Letters 164 [56] and 167 [58], respectively, of 17 February 1807 and 23 March 1807. Being with the French army probably did let him visit otherwise inaccessible areas.[5]

4 Jean Tulard, *Napoléon ou le mythe du sauveur* (Paris: Fayard (Collection Pluriel), 1987), 42–4, 461.

5 Others too emphasized that they were both soldiers and sightseers. Thus, the reserve officer, Victor de Musset-Pathay, declares: 'ma manière donc, inconnue

Alongside those incidental benefits of serving in Italy, had Courier any motives connected with the essence of soldiering? Perhaps patriotism, but it does not appear in his letters. On the contrary, such an honourable reason seems to be excluded by certain passages on the futility of soldiering. In the letter to Klewanski which praises the joys of Italy for the scholar, he calls his duties 'folies tantôt barbares, tantôt ridicules, auxquelles je prends part sans savoir pourquoi' (136 [40], 10 June 1806, *CG* I, 231). And later he wrote to Mme Pigalle: 'Imaginez un peu à quoi je passe mon temps. Je rêve nuit et jour aux moyens de tuer des gens que je n'ai jamais vus, qui ne m'ont fait ni bien ni mal' (145 [51], 10 September 1806, *CG* I, 254). Here, less abstractly than to Klewanski, he presents his activity as gratuitous killing. But, while the killing lacks any personal justification for Courier, it clearly serves his masters' political purposes: 'nous prenons un petit royaume pour la dynastie impériale' (ibid.). Courier was in fact especially dubious about wars of conquest, as appears obliquely in his jocular, often ironic references to himself as a conqueror. His ironies, to which we shall often refer, usually have a tripartite structure: a surface meaning, an underlying, divergent meaning, and some indication that the underlying meaning is the principal sense. Thus, he lauds ironically the 'bonté adorable' with which enemy armies surrender, 'ce qui encourage dans le métier de conquérant. Sans cela on y renoncerait' (132 [37], April 1806, *CG* I, 225). The same letter refers to Napoleon's ambitions, which he had furthered by making his brother Joseph King of Naples in place of the Bourbon Ferdinando IV. In 1806, Joseph was trying to assert his authority over Sicily, which was still in Ferdinando's power. According to Courier,

> toute l'Italie n'est rien pour moi, si je n'y joins la Sicile. Ce que j'en dis c'est pour soutenir mon caractère de conquérant. Car entre nous, je me soucie peu que la Sicile paye ses taxes à Joseph ou à Ferdinand. (*CG* I, 224)

Here mock bombast turns into derision of himself and of the Bonapartes' fiscal appetites. Meanwhile, in a letter written probably to Clavier, he claims that current wars do not deserve historians' attention, for 'c'est

---

jusqu'à moi, c'est de voyager avec une *armée*' (Gilles Bertrand, *Le Grand Tour revisité* (Rome: École française de Rome, 2013), ch. 9, p. 9).

sottise de méditer sur ce qui dépend des digestions de B …'; and referring anew to the frivolity of those who decide between peace and war, Courier adds: 'Tout tient au caprice de deux ou trois bipèdes sans plumes qui se jouent de l'espèce humaine' (126 [30], … 1805, *CG* I, 215–16). The featherless bipeds are from ancient Greece: Plato having defined man as a being with two legs and no feathers, Diogenes the Cynic mocked his definition by displaying a plucked fowl as Plato's man.[6] Though the laughable bipeds, without feathers and implicitly without reason, include other leaders besides Napoleon, he is the one named target. These dismissive remarks in 1805 and 1806 came when the aim of French foreign policy was changing from defence of the Revolutionary transformation to promotion of Napoleon's dynastic ambitions.[7]

Despite his misgivings, Courier never disowns war in itself. This is usual enough amongst French thinkers of liberal tendency, as exemplified by Constant. For him, war of self-defence was evidently justified, but he too has misgivings about other wars. As we have seen, he thought that war, like trade, had been a way for a nation to obtain goods that it wanted. In earlier times men had naturally fought over scarce resources. But now society has evolved away from war, because men have come to prize peaceful enjoyment of their possessions: 'avec le repos l'aisance, et comme source de l'aisance, l'industrie'; and also because experience shows that no state can dominate its neighbours indefinitely:

> l'époque du commerce […] doit nécessairement remplacer celle de la guerre […] La guerre et le commerce ne sont que deux moyens différents d'arriver au même but: celui de posséder ce que l'on désire. Le commerce […] est une tentative pour obtenir de gré à gré ce qu'on n'espère plus conquérir par la violence.[8]

De l'esprit de conquête was not published until 1814. As for Courier, then, his thinking on the futility of the pro-dynastic war in which he is

6 Diogenes Laërtius, *Lives and Opinions of Eminent Philosophers* (Cambridge, MA: Harvard U. P. (Loeb Classical Library), 1925), vol. 6, ch. 2, p. 40.

7 Tulard, *Napoléon*, 185–8.

8 *De l'esprit de conquête* in *Écrits politiques*, 130–1.

involved is sketchy, but it somewhat resembles, and certainly anticipates, Constant's assessment.[9]

Did Courier aspire to martial glory? Probably not, though many pursued this prize.[10] He assures M. Dansse de Villoison: 'J'en étais un peu dégoûté, de la gloire, par de certaines gens que j'en vois couverts de la tête aux pieds, et qui n'en ont pas meilleur air.' Glory is lavished on soldiers so indiscriminately that it becomes meaningless, unlike the unique distinction of the learned translator which Dansse de Villoison urges him to pursue. The latter form of glory attracts Courier: 'puisque vous dites que moi seul je puis cueillir de pareils lauriers [...] A mes yeux, honneurs et plaisirs, par cette qualité d'exclusifs acquièrent un grand prix' (101 [26], 27 February 1805, *CG* I, 177–8). Even as a source of renown, then, soldiering interests Courier less than the study of antiquity. However, despite his scepticism, he did acknowledge that military glory was sometimes well earned. Thus, he criticizes Bonaparte's wish to become Emperor: 'le premier capitaine du monde, vouloir qu'on l'appelle Majesté. Etre Bonaparte et se faire Sire! [...] Il aime mieux un titre qu'un nom. Pauvre homme' (71 [23], 1804, *CG* I, 143). His wish is pitiful precisely because his glory is merited.

Courier's more general views on war, which centre on the Calabrian guerrilla campaign, are reflected in his letters of 1806–7. He recounts certain events at second hand as when, in describing an ambush, he explains that he is narrating a representative composite of various encounters, an 'esquisse des scènes qui s'y passent à présent' (132 [37], April 1806, *CG* I, 225). But sometimes he gives no such indication and simply uses 'nous' as if he had been present, even when he had not, for example, at the battle of Maida, which he reports in Letter 146 [48]. In such cases, 'nous' presumably means 'notre armée'. Though such ambiguity in some of Courier's reports is unfortunate, he remains at least an informed commentator. A first, basic question is the legality of the campaign against the irregulars who

9 Constant's *Journaux intimes*, from December 1813 onwards, reveal his impatience to publish *De l'esprit de conquête* and thus impress Bernadotte, a possible successor to Napoleon (Benjamin Constant, *Œuvres*, ed. Alfred Roulin (Paris: Gallimard (Pléiade), 1957), 687–91).

10 Jean-Claude Damamme, *Les Soldats de la Grande Armée* (Paris: Perrin, 1998), 121–30.

continued to resist after French forces routed the Neapolitan army in March 1806. The official French position was that resistance by inhabitants of occupied territory was inherently criminal, and punishable under the *Code pénal militaire*:

> La révolte, la sédition ou la désobéissance combinée de la part des habitans du pays ennemi occupé par les troupes de la république, seront punies de mort, soit que la désobéissance se soit manifestée contre les chefs militaires, soit que la révolte ou sédition ait été dirigée contre tout ou partie des troupes de la république.
>
> Sera puni de la même peine tout habitant du pays ennemi convaincu d'avoir excité le mouvement de révolte, sédition ou désobéissance, quand même il n'y aurait pas autrement pris part, ou que ses efforts pour l'exciter auraient été sans succès. (Titre VIII, Art 4)

A more specific text is a decree issued on 31 July 1806 by Joseph Bonaparte as 'roi de Naples et de Sicile'.[11] The enactment was necessary because Joseph's kingdom was within the Empire and no longer a 'pays ennemi occupé'. His decree confirmed the criminality of irregulars but did require the trial of alleged transgressors by 'commissions militaires' (Arts III, IX). This requirement was sometimes flouted and many who were duly tried were executed: between 1 April 1806 and 1 March 1807, the military court in Cosenza sentenced 57% to death and acquitted 15%; implicitly, the remaining 28% were imprisoned or sentenced to hard labour.[12] Though an acquittal rate of 15% may not be high, it shows that trial by *commission militaire* gave some protection to the accused and that French repression of irregular resistance was not wholly arbitrary.

But Courier himself was sceptical about such treatment of irregulars. He describes to another officer an episode which he had witnessed:

> nous pendîmes un capucin à San Giovanni in Fiore, et une vingtaine de pauvres diables qui avaient plus la mine de charbonniers que d'autre chose. Le capucin, homme d'esprit, parla fort bien à Reynier. Reynier lui disait: vous avez prêché contre nous. Il s'en défendit. Ses raisons me paraissaient assez bonnes. Nous voyant partis en gens

11 *Journal de l'Empire*, 22 August 1806, p. 1.

12 Nicolas Cadet, 'Anatomie d'une "petite guerre", la campagne de Calabre de 1806–1807', *Revue d'histoire du XIXe siècle*, 30 (2005), on line, 12. The dates imply that the tribunals were active before Joseph's decree was published.

> qui ne devaient pas revenir, il avait prêché pour ceux à qui nous cédions la place. Pouvait-il faire autrement? Mais si on les écoutait, on ne pendrait personne. (142 [45], August 1806 *CG* I, 249)

The friar is accused of inciting hostility to the French. His defence, as summarized by Courier, is essentially that he acted under duress: 'Pouvait-il faire autrement?' But this defence fails because, as Courier observes: 'si on les écoutait, on ne pendrait personne'. In short, General Reynier was determined to hang suspects in order to intimidate, and punishing illegality was a secondary concern. We may note in passing that the fate of the 'pauvres diables' in San Giovanni in Fiore is an early and extreme example of the oppression of the humble which Courier later condemned in France.

While Courier clearly thought duress a fair excuse in the friar's case, a prior question is whether resistance or inciting resistance were really crimes at all. Without discussing the point explicitly, Courier hints at an opinion. First, there is the general remark: 'si on les écoutait, on ne pendrait personne'. This suggests that, even if resistance were really illegal, there would always be a viable excuse for it, that the offence would remain theoretical and the attendant penalties unenforceable. More specifically, his scepticism may arise at least partly from the French *Code* itself, which applies to any 'pays ennemi occupé par les troupes de la république'. If fomenting resistance to the French is an offence when they are in occupation, it presumably ceases to be an offence when they withdraw. Certainly, Courier seems to invite this conclusion in noting that, for the friar, the French having left hastily, the true occupying power was rather 'ceux à qui nous cédions la place'. It might of course be argued that, by August 1806, the French army's authority derived rather from Joseph's decree than the *Code*, but Courier probably doubted Joseph's own authority to issue decrees. This doubt emerges obliquely when he describes the fate of the marchese di Rodìo, one of Ferdinando's officers, who had been 'pris dans un recoin de la Calabre à la tête de quelques insurgés'. A *commission militaire*, under political pressure, condemned him and he was executed on 25 April 1806: 'On le fusilla par derrière comme traître, félon, rebelle à son *légitime* souverain. Le trait vous paraît fort' (179 [65], July 1807, *CG* I, 305).[13] Courier's emphasis suggests

13 Thierry Lentz, *Joseph Bonaparte* (Paris: Perrin, 2016), 365–78.

that he was most struck, or shocked, by the assertion of Joseph's legitimacy. And if he doubted Joseph's legitimacy as ruler, then he necessarily doubted the authority of Joseph's decrees, including the decree against irregular resistance. Finally, we may also note, tentatively, Courier's very silence on the legality or illegality of resistance. As a rule, it is unsafe to place an interpretation on mere silence, but his silence about irregular resistance as such may have some significance because he certainly does underline the cruelty or criminal origins of some insurgents. However, he never says that the irregulars in general are criminal simply by being insurgents. In this regard, he makes no distinction in principle between irregulars and regular troops. In its day, that was a remarkable stance. Seventy years were to pass before an international conference even tried to legalize the position of irregulars: the Brussels Declaration of August 1874 (Articles 9 and 10) would have given them legal rights and duties akin to those of regular forces, but the Declaration was not ratified, and its principles were only adopted in the Hague Convention of 1899 (Ch. I, arts 1 and 2).

For some historians, the uprising involved all Calabrians and was inspired by patriotism and religious fervour.[14] This interpretation is sometimes supported, sometimes contradicted, by letters in which Courier touches on the irregulars' origins and motives. Here a significant question concerns the sense in which the insurgents are 'criminal': are they common criminals, or criminals only as defined by French military law? As regards Courier's terminology, he sometimes calls the insurgents collectively 'paysans', insurgés' or 'montagnards', using neutral, non-pejorative terms which impute no criminality to them. But what of the cases when he uses nouns which would be pejorative in ordinary usage, for example, 'brigand', 'brigandage', or 'bandit'? Occasionally, the men to whom he applies these terms are plainly common criminals. Thus, on the dearth of country houses round Barletta, he explains that 'les brigands rendent la campagne inhabitable' (107 [29], 23

14 Tulard, *Napoléon*, 393. On Courier's Calabria, Lautman, 89–93. On the campaign: Christopher Duggan, *The Force of Destiny: A History of Italy since 1796* (London: Penguin Books, 2008), 54–6; Nicolas Cadet, 'Anatomie d'une "petite guerre"', 30; Sandro Petrucci, 'Opposizione popolare, insorgenza e brigantaggio nell'Italia napoleonica', *Annali di storia moderna e contemporanea*, 14 (2008), 259–86. Lentz, *Joseph Bonaparte*, 370–3.

April 1805, *CG* I, 189). But most French soldiers used 'brigands' to refer to all irregulars, whether or not they were tainted with common criminality. This habit can create ambiguity in Courier's letters to other soldiers: if he uses 'brigands', he may mean either, narrowly, mere criminals, or, broadly, all insurgents, in the sense of 'brigand' familiar to his correspondent. The broad sense is more likely, but the narrow one can occur, as when he jokes to a colleague that 'il y avait dans ce pays-ci beaucoup de brigands, même avant que nous y vinssions' (164 [56], February 1807, *CG* I, 285).[15]

That said, Courier's use of 'paysans' as a collective term probably implies that he took many irregulars to be simply peasants (e.g. Letter 146 [48], 2 October 1806, *CG* I, 256). This reading is supported by passages in which 'paysans' are listed separately from manifest criminals. For instance, the ambush mentioned above involves a band, 'tant paysans que bandits, forçats déchaînés, déserteurs, commandés par un sous-diacre' (132 [37] *CG* I, 226). Courier seems to distinguish here between non-criminal guerrillas ('paysans') and others, who are all more or less criminal in their origins. The deserters were from Joseph's reconstituted Neapolitan army; the 'forçats' were convicts whom the British had freed.[16] Elsewhere, he complains of his difficulties with 'les insurgés sur ma route, les brigands de toute espèce' (137 [41], 1806, *CG* I, 235). As he differentiates 'insurgés' from 'brigands', we may again infer that the 'insurgés' are non-criminal in origin. These cases suggest that Courier tries to distinguish between types of insurgent and does not lump them all together as criminals. Such distinctions imply both lucidity and fairness of mind.

As for the insurgents' motives, Courier mentions several strands. Religious fervour seems indeed to have played a part, as when he and his men were almost killed in a village where the faithful 'animés par leurs prêtres, voulurent faire la bonne œuvre de nous assassiner' (107 [29], 23 April 1805, *CG* I, 187). Clerical leadership is also exemplified by the subdeacon whose band is mentioned in Letter 132 [37]. Patriotism, meaning loyalty to King Ferdinando, was another major factor. Typically, Cardinal

15 On soldiers' usage, Cadet, 'Anatomie d'une "petite guerre"', 2. Petrucci tends to stress that French use of 'brigand' is denigration ('Opposizione popolare', 263–5). The word is indeed disparaging, but it also reflects French military law.

16 *CG* I, 226, n. 19.

Ruffo, the leader of a previous anti-French uprising in 1799, had summoned Calabrians to defend both their religion and their legitimate sovereign.[17] However, some truly criminal gangs of thieves and highwaymen may have had perverse reasons for loyalty to the Bourbons. Even in times of peace, such gangs were active enough to make the kingdom of Naples insecure, as Courier complains in Letters 104 [27], 164 [56] or 167 [58]. In short, they benefited from the laxity of the Bourbon government. Some had also earned an advantageous role during Ruffo's campaign. We read that 'ceux qui se distinguèrent alors par leurs brigandages sont aujourd'hui les favoris du gouvernement qui les emploie à lever des contributions' (107 [29], 23 April 1805, *CG* I, 186). Courier also records that the Bourbons used gangs of criminals as what we might call militias: 'Tout le pays est plein de brigands par la faute du gouvernement qui se sert d'eux pour vexer et piller ses propres sujets' (ibid.). Whether the Bourbons simply tolerated them or employed them, such brigands had a direct stake in the status quo and a strong incentive to become insurgents. In reality, patriotism can of course coexist with other motives, but here Courier is emphasizing a murky alliance between these particular brigands and the Bourbon monarchy. The final important motive for resistance is French soldiers' misconduct, such as looting: 'Imaginez comme on nous aime', as he writes to M. de Sainte-Croix. In this connection, he can invoke personal experience of moments when the behaviour of Italian children betrays their parents' real feelings of fear and hatred towards the French: 'Dans la maison où l'on me faisait l'accueil le plus flatteur, j'ai toujours vu les enfants que je voulais caresser me repousser avec horreur' (146 [48], 2 October 1806, *CG* I, 257–8). In addition to looting, other military atrocities caused and exasperated local outrage. In reprisal for ambushes, a French commander 's'en prend aux villages voisins [...] on pille, on viole, on égorge'; the result is not that ambushes stop, but rather that 'ce qui échappe va grossir la bande du sous-diacre' (132 [37], April 1806, *CG* I, 226). Courier's remarks on the harm done to the French army by such barbarities seem quite enlightened. Though the policy of repression succeeded militarily, it required two more years.[18]

17 Duggan, 21–3.

18 Petrucci, 'Opposizione popolare', 282–6.

Whatever his doubts about the provisions of French legislation and his lucidity about the conduct of French troops, Courier also saw clearly the evils of the irregulars. As we have noted, he was aware that material gain motivated some of them. But above all, he records their sadism. When French troops are ambushed, 'les plus heureux meurent sur place; les autres durant quelques jours servent de jouet à leurs bourreaux' (132 [37], *CG* I, 226). The practice of burning captured Frenchmen alive brings together cruelty and religious fervour, as is implied by the term 'auto-da-fé' in the report of events in Strongoli: 'Nous trouvâmes là six canonniers du régiment, dans un cachot [...]. On les gardait pour un petit *auto-da-fé*' (147 [49], 1806, *CG* I, 266). Courier generally presents such cruelty with restraint; here, the tongue-in-cheek use of 'petit' minimizes the horror of the plan. In the same faintly jocular vein, he writes of the exchanges of atrocities between the French army and the irregulars: 'Nous les pendons; ils nous brûlent le plus doucement qu'ils peuvent et nous font quelquefois l'honneur de nous manger' (148 [50], 15 October 1806, *CG* I, 269).

Though critical of the guerrillas' cruelty, Courier appreciated that they were generally willing fighters, unlike various regular armies, to whose 'bonté adorable' he refers ironically (132 [37], *CG* I, 225). It may be unfair to suggest cowardice, but stunning French triumphs in 1805 at Ulm and Austerlitz discouraged opposition for a time. By recalling easy successes against regular troops, Courier highlights both the contrasting difficulty of fighting Calabrian irregulars and also the deficiencies of the French army, which are revealed by the typical ambush:

> un détachement d'une centaine de nos gens en désordre [...] Au pied de la hauteur coule un torrent rapide qu'il faut passer pour arriver sur l'autre montée. Partie de la file est déjà dans l'eau, partie en deçà, au delà. Tout à coup se lèvent de différents côtés mille tant paysans que bandits [...] commandés par un sous-diacre, bien armés, bons tireurs, ils font feu sur les nôtres avant d'en être vus. (132 [37], April 1806, *CG* I, 225–6)

As the attack is well coordinated, the band is clearly disciplined and capably led. These irregulars are fitted for this kind of fighting, being 'bons tireurs' who can rely on individual marksmanship. The French party, on the other hand, having been allowed to string out, is dispersed as well as outnumbered. The soldiers' position is no doubt irretrievable, because most infantry units had to concentrate in column or line to produce effective fire.

According to the same letter, the French perform poorly in such cases because officers ignore the threat of insurgent activity: 'Prendre des précautions, se garder, à quoi bon? Depuis plus de huit jours il n'y a point eu de troupe massacrée dans le canton' (*CG* I, 226). Courier associates the French commanders' negligence with their exclusive interest in loot and women:

> le général [...] a fait partir ce détachement sans songer à rien, sans savoir la plupart du temps si les passages étaient libres [...] à quoi s'occupe ce commandant dans son cantonnement? S'il est jeune, il cherche des filles; s'il est vieux, il amasse de l'argent. Souvent il prend de l'un et de l'autre; la guerre ne se fait que pour cela. (Ibid.)

While the last sentence implies that such priorities were usual in the French army, Courier thought that officers became greedier as they rose in rank. Thus, he writes acidly to an unnamed colleague awaiting promotion: 'on vous promet [...] quelque province échappée aux Brune et aux Masséna, après lesquels vous ne vouliez pas glaner dans les grades inférieurs, vous sentant fait pour moissonner à pleines mains aussi bien qu'eux'.[19] Like their officers, the ordinary soldiers are greedy for plunder, and almost blind to the fate of their comrades captured by guerrillas: 'Chacun espère s'en tirer avec son fourgon plein, ou ses mulets chargés, et se moque de tout le reste' (132 [37], April 1806, *CG* I, 225).[20] Generalized looting, when the soldiers put pillage before all else, caused discipline to collapse. But Courier recognized that the rankers' behaviour also came of necessity, for they lacked supplies. Thus, he writes of the desperate retreat from Maida, when the soldiers mutinied: 'Enfin nos soldats se révoltèrent et tirèrent sur leurs

19 *Conseils à un colonel*, *OC*, 570. This piece might be considered an early pamphlet but is included here for its epistolary form and thematic links to undisputedly genuine letters. On Masséna, see Philip Dwyer, *Napoleon: The Path to Power 1769–1799* (London: Bloomsbury, 2007), 225, and Damamme, 536, n. 8.

20 Unauthorized looting was in law a capital offence (*Code pénal militaire*, Titre V, Art. 1), but in practice was largely tolerated (Damamme, 67; Dwyer, *Napoleon*, 201–3).

officiers. L'habitude du pillage, unique moyen de subsister, avait détruit toute discipline' (146 [48], 2 October 1806, *CG* I, 256).

Along with their own greed for loot, Courier identifies two causes of officers' laxity. First, undue faith in Napoleon. He writes ironically to General Dulauloy: 'Je sais bien [...] qu'avec le génie de l'empereur nous vaincrons toujours et partout, quelque faute que nous puissions faire. Mais un peu de bon sens, d'ordre, de prévoyance, ne nuiraient à rien' (135 [38], *CG* I, 230). The other cause of laxity is a courtier mentality, which distracts officers from their duties. Thus, Courier's commander Reynier, surrounded by sycophantic juniors, listens exclusively to flatterers (138 [42],1806, *CG* I, 237). Only after defeat at Maida does he come to his senses: 'le voilà raisonnable, abordable. On lui parle; il écoute à présent' (140 [43], August 1806, *CG* I, 238). A related weakness is, according to Courier, the failure to promote capable junior officers, of whom there is no lack. As he writes to M. de Sainte-Croix: 'Il y a toujours dans une armée cent officiers capables de la bien commander' (190 [72], 27 November 1807, *CG* I, 318). But they are not usually promoted because, in the current climate, preferment goes to the most servile; Courier ascribes his own lack of promotion to his being a 'mauvais courtisan' (229 [89], 13 September 1808, *CG* II, 45). The *Conseils à un colonel* gives a still more damning explanation for the mediocrity of French leadership. Courier asserts that a commander appointing his own subordinates will choose none who might outshine him:

> toutes les fois que, selon l'usage des armées romaines, *vir virum legit* [each chooses his own man], personne ne s'associe un plus vaillant que soi [...] d'où il arrive nécessairement que les meilleurs restent en bas, faute de quelqu'un qui leur tende la main. (*OC*, 576)

Courier may himself have experienced the practices which he describes here, but they were certainly not universal in the French army: Bonaparte, on the contrary, advanced such a dashing subordinate as Ney.

Though Courier's various manners as a letter-writer are not our main concern here, it is still worth noting that, on the same subject, he can write in divergent styles, respectively, to soldiers and to scholars. An example is his dismissal of military glory in letters to another officer, presumably Poydavant, and to the scholar Dansse de Villoison. He writes to the former:

> Il faut se payer de lauriers qui heureusement coûtent peu. Pour moi, j'en quitte ma part. J'ai la gloire *in culo* comme disent les Italiens, ou plus poliment *in tasca*, depuis que j'entendis quelqu'un de notre connaissance dire: *je suis couvert de gloire*, et les courtisans répéter *il est couvert de gloire*. (122 [34], 28 November 1805, *CG* I, 209–10)

Courier's disdain for glory emerges notably from bringing together a noble term, 'lauriers', and a dismissive vulgarity, 'in culo'. His contempt is explained, not by principle, but by irritation with 'quelqu'un de notre connaissance' and especially with his flatterers. These characters are dramatized economically by an exchange of noble clichés, in which 'quelqu'un' praises himself and the courtiers, thus prompted, mechanically echo his words. This attack *ad hominem* relies of course on shared knowledge of the targets and implies complicity between Courier and Poydavant.

To Dansse de Villoison, Courier writes, in a passage quoted already: 'J'en étais un peu dégoûté, de la gloire, par de certaines gens que j'en vois couverts de la tête aux pieds et qui n'en ont pas meilleur air' (101 [26], 27 February 1805, *CG* I, 177). Courier's reaction is conveyed partly by ironic understatement: he is 'un peu dégoûté'; those who are glorified 'n'en ont pas meilleur air', probably because their glory is palpably usurped. As for the targets, Dansse de Villoison would probably not have known them; thus, in calling them 'de certaines gens', Courier is making a show of discretion. We have then two versions of the same point: one, energetic in expression and suggesting familiarity between Courier and his correspondent; the other more reserved and ironic in its terms. Such letters display fine control of differing tones, which no doubt imply a sense of what is appropriate to the recipient, to the 'audience'. As for the irony which appears here and, as we have seen, in various other letters, it was to become a notable feature of the pamphlets.

A good many of Courier's letters, then, deal lucidly and independently with various matters of substance.[21] His scepticism about military glory, about wars of conquest, and about Napoleon is unusual for the period, but his view of the fighting in Calabria is most remarkable, for he conveys that

21 But Auerbach thought the letters 'fast ohne Substanz und Inhalt, ganz ohne Gesinnung' (p. 518).

the irregulars and the French are similar, at least in misconduct. There are common criminals amongst the insurgents, but also in the French army, as witnessed by the incidence of looting. The two sides are equally barbarous in trading horror for horror: summary hanging for burning and cannibalism (148 [50], 15 October 1806, *CG* I, 269). For a French officer, it was most unorthodox to see his own army as no better than such opponents.[22] His impartiality towards the insurgents has won admiration in Italy and, on this point, we may leave the last word to Leonardo Sciascia who underlines that Courier 'mai li mette su un piano morale diverso da quello in cui lui e Massena e l'esercito della repubblica francese si muovono'.[23]

22 French soldiers usually disdained Italians, whom they considered 'perfides, rusés, peu travailleurs, cruels, irréfléchis, prompts à jouer du stylet, jaloux, superstitieux' (Bertrand, ch. 9, p. 12).

23 Leonardo Sciascia, 'Brigantaggio napoletano e mafia siciliana', in *Opere*, ed. Paolo Squillacioti, 3 vols (Milan: Adelphi Edizioni, 2012–19), vol. 2, pp. 301–7 (p. 302).

CHAPTER 2

Pamphlets, 1816–1820: Essential Priorities

Courier's first clearly political piece, the *Pétition aux deux Chambres* of December 1816 is both a pamphlet and also a true petition, of which copies were sent to members of the legislature.[1] The episodes in question belong to the months of repression by Louis XVIII's government after Napoleon's return from exile and defeat at Waterloo. The *Pétition* is initially about some villagers arrested in Luynes. Apart from defending the accused, the pamphlet has four targets: abuse of position by such figures as the mayor or the priest (*OC*, 4–5, 7; *Éc*, 125–6, 128), the gendarmerie (*OC*, 5; *Éc*, 126), supine judges (*OC*, 6–7; *Éc*, 127), and the authoritarian laws. The argument moves thus from the villagers to an appeal for legislative change; the movement from particular to general helps underline that the individual cases exemplify a disorder affecting all France.[2]

Those detained were allegedly Bonapartists plotting against the monarchy. According to Courier, the charges were necessarily groundless, for the accused were apolitical: 'peu de gens chez nous savent ce que c'est que le gouvernement' (*OC*, 4; *Éc*, 125). The arrests are also arbitrary by their inconsistency: one villager, Georges Mauclair, is detained for five to six weeks for having supposedly 'mal parlé [...] du gouvernement' (ibid.); another is left undisturbed, despite saying publicly that 'il gardait son vin pour le vendre au retour de Bonaparte, ajoutant qu'il n'attendrait guère' (ibid.). Courier attributes these disparities to villagers' personal relations with the local potentates, who 'voient toujours dans leurs ennemis les ennemis du roi' (*OC*, 7; *Éc*, 128). There is, then, a local reign of terror that is no less terrifying for being local, since it exploits harsh laws designed to protect

1 Crouzet, *Éc*, 118.

2 The *Pétition* appeared after most of the accused had been freed (Lautman, 157–8). Obviously, the broader issues remained.

the whole state. But the security laws are only tools. Recalling caustically the persecution of protestants in earlier centuries, Courier writes: 'on eût aussi bien fait de nous brûler comme entachés de l'hérésie de nos ancêtres, que de nous déporter ou nous emprisonner comme séditieux' (*OC*, 9; *Éc*, 130). In short, if the security legislation had been unavailable, other laws would have been used. Courier's main point is that Luynes suffers from mayoral tyranny and, implicitly, that such local despotism may exist anywhere in France. Tyrannical mayors became a recurrent theme in his writing: a striking example appears in an imaginary letter from a victim about to flee the area (*Gazette*, *OC*, 187–9; *Éc*, 423–5.)

The chief servants of oppression are the gendarmes, whose powers over ordinary subjects are largely unchecked. Courier remarks in an aside: 'L'autorité, messieurs, voilà le grand mot en France. Ailleurs, on dit la loi, ici l'autorité [...] celle des gendarmes' (*OC*, 5; *Éc*, 126). The aside confirms that this pamphlet concerns wrongs afflicting not only Luynes, but all of France. The gendarmerie's power is not merely an abstract institutional issue, for the gendarme is a very material figure of fear. Thus, one detainee's daughter suffers a fatal shock: 'Cette nuit, ces gendarmes, et son père enchaîné, ne s'effaçaient point de sa mémoire [...] depuis quinze jours elle est morte' (*OC*, 6; *Éc*, 126–7). The psychological impact of intimidatory, intrusive policing was another of Courier's lasting preoccupations. In 1823 he complained that 'la police est le plus puissant de tous les moyens inventés pour rendre un peuple vil et lâche. Quel courage peut avoir l'homme élevé dans la peur des gendarmes ?' (*Livret*, *OC*, 167; *Éc*, 402).

Courier's third target is the judiciary. The courts should have protected the guiltless villagers but, according to Courier, that could not happen. He says of the prisoners that

> entre ceux qui les accusaient et ceux qui devaient les juger comme bonapartistes, ils se trouvaient les seuls peut-être qui n'eussent point juré fidélité à Bonaparte [...] Le magistrat qui les poursuit avec tant de rigueur aujourd'hui, sous prétexte de bonapartisme, traitait de même leurs enfants [...] pour avoir refusé de servir Bonaparte. (*OC*, 6–7; *Éc*,127)

These judges and prosecutors, after serving Napoleon zealously, appear to have changed sides diametrically. But in appearance only, for in reality they have not changed at all: throughout, they have sided with the political powers. Indifferent to justice, such judges will obviously not protect anyone from the local executive. As Courier says, the villagers have been 'réduits au désespoir par ces magistrats mêmes, leurs naturels appuis' (*OC*, 10; *Éc*, 130).

The final major target of the *Pétition* is the current legislation. Implicitly, a petition to the legislature seeks legislative change. Courier does not offer explicit proposals but, since his grievances include the excesses of overweening office-holders such as mayors, he is implicitly seeking legislation to restrain them. At the time, proceedings against an office-holder were allowed only if the Conseil d'État gave permission, meaning in practice that there was no legal redress against misuse of office by country's mayors.[3] Constant had tried to correct this anomaly via the *Acte additionnel* to Napoleon's constitution of 1815, but the attempt collapsed with Napoleon's second abdication, and only in 1870 was a decree issued to remedy the situation.[4] Courier's implicit appeal to the legislature places him then somewhat ahead of his time. Overall, the pamphlet highlights two connected ideas which he upheld consistently: individual freedom depends both on protective legislation, and on the integrity of those applying the legislation. The *Pétition* is also a good example of his ability to connect very localized wrongs and the institutional shortcomings that facilitated them. What might just have been an account of pitiful victims being crushed by local tyrants becomes a notable argument for measures to protect the freedoms of the subject. Characteristically, the protagonists are modest, but they are named individuals. Such use of names reflects Courier's interest in the particular, and will reappear in later pamphlets.

In 1819 Courier started a succession of political pamphlets, the *Lettres au 'Censeur'* (1819–20) and the *Lettres particulières* (1820). The *Censeur européen*, as it was known in 1819, was a periodical of liberal sympathies which published eight of Courier's ten letters (I–VII and IX). All ten appeared subsequently in the collected *Lettres au rédacteur du 'Censeur', par*

3 Constitution of 22 frimaire, an VIII (13 December 1799), Article 75 (Rials, 36–7). Constant, *Principes de politique*, in *Écrits politiques*, 421–2.

4 Rials, 47, n. 1.

P.-L. Courier, cultivateur (1820). The two *Lettres particulières* appeared later in 1820 as individual pamphlets. The *Lettres au 'Censeur'* concern several of Courier's major interests, notably national independence, personal freedom, press freedom, the royal court, and the defence of smallholding. The *Lettres particulières* touch on some of the same questions, but also the loyalties of the army. Both sets of *Lettres* differ slightly in perspective from the *Pétition*: the *Pétition* raised national issues, but its origins were local; the *Lettres* deal more directly with national questions.

These pamphlets were produced in a situation made fraught by two chronic political issues and two significant events. One chronic question centred on estates which, having belonged until 1789 to nobles or the Church, had been confiscated by the Revolution and designated *biens nationaux*. Many such estates had subsequently been divided and sold off as smallholdings. The Consulat had restored their property to some *émigré* nobles who had returned to France, but other nobles and the Church had not recovered their estates.[5] The question of ownership was theoretically closed because article 9 of the *Charte* protected the new proprietors. But in practice those former owners who had not regained their property went on demanding its return, and *restitution* remained a contentious matter although they were compensated from public funds in 1825.[6] A second persistent issue was the role of the Sainte Alliance, which kept armies in France until November 1818 and continued thereafter to exert pressure on Louis's government. The influence exerted by the Allies, especially Austria and Russia, was highly conservative because they feared popular unrest in France or elsewhere.[7]

Against this background, the first major event was the murder in February 1820 of Louis XVIII's nephew, the duc de Berry. The murderer, the Bonapartist Louis-Pierre Louvel, hoped to extinguish the Bourbon

5 Tulard, *Les Français sous Napoléon*, 77–8.

6 Bertier, 372–5; Alfred Cobban, *History of Modern France*, 3 vols (Harmondsworth: Penguin Books, 1961–5), vol. 2, pp. 85–6.

7 Bertier, 174–5. On his neutrality in the Greek War of Independence, the Czar allegedly declared: 'Pour l'intérêt de mon peuple et de ma religion, je devais faire la guerre au Turc; mais j'ai cru voir qu'il s'agissait de révolution entre la Grèce et le Turc, je n'ai point fait la guerre' (*Livret*, *OC*, 168; *Éc*, 403).

dynasty, for Berry was the one man in the ageing royal family capable of fathering heirs to the throne. As he had no sons at the time, the French Bourbon line did indeed seem doomed. In fact, the Duchess was pregnant and bore a son in September, but in February few knew of her pregnancy. Berry's death provoked extreme reactions, as when the ultra député Jean-Claude Clausel de Coussergues tried to prosecute the minister Decazes for complicity in the murder. His initiative came to nothing, but the very attempt suggests the climate in which the legislature adopted new repressive measures, such as press censorship (March 1820).[8] But, as we shall see, Courier thought that some of the legislation owed more to dictation by the Allies than to decisions by Louis's ministers. The other major event was the legislative election of November 1820. In May–June 1820, the electoral law was amended. The old legislation provided for 258 députés, and an electorate of men paying at least 300 francs in annual direct taxes. The new law raised the number of députés to 430: 258 to be elected as before; the extra 172 to be elected by one-quarter of the electors in each department, those paying the highest direct taxes. The richest could thus vote twice, which favoured conservative candidates, as did royalist sentiment, intensified by the fate of Berry and the birth of his son.[9] The new government was likely to be reactionary.

We may begin with Courier's views on the *biens nationaux*, of which the sale in modest lots had transformed many landless peasants into smallholders. Courier recognized that these last did not always prosper, that their life was hard, and that some literally worked themselves to death (e.g. *Gazette*, *OC*, 178; *Éc*, 415). But in general, he stresses that the benefits were great. His main defence of smallholding appears slightly later in the *Simple Discours*. But it is foreshadowed here by a spokesman, a no doubt imaginary neighbour, according to whom increased smallholding promotes wealth, personal morality, and public order: 'On travaille mieux et plus. Or, avec plus de travail, il y a plus de produits [...] plus de mœurs, plus d'ordre dans l'État comme dans les familles. Tout vice vient d'oisiveté,

8 Ministerial policy was already growing more repressive, and the murder encouraged this trend (Bertier, 163–6; Price, 106–9).

9 Bertier, 169–72.

tout désordre public vient du manque de travail' (*Lcens.* V, *OC*, 19; *Éc*, 190–1). This defence of land redistribution is utilitarian in spirit: it concerns more or less tangible benefits for the greatest number, rather than seeing redistribution as a matter of social justice. As for morality, pursuit of the antithesis between idleness and work probably led to an overstatement of Courier's position, for he recognizes in the *Simple Discours* that vice is not always due to idleness. But clearly, he believed that enlightened self-interest can promote order and morality. Though the idea may seem trite, it was pertinent to current debates. Implicitly, it met the contention that Christianity was necessary for orderly life in society: Catholic priests, largely ousted during the early years of the century, often asserted that morality had declined in their absence;[10] and many laymen whose world-picture had been shaped before the Revolution agreed that Christianity played a major social role. Thus, Chateaubriand urged religious revival, arguing that in pagan Antiquity slavery had preserved order but, when men are free, only Christianity can ensure morality and social order:

> qui réprimera une masse énorme de paysans libres et éloignés de l'œil du magistrat [...] si ce n'est une religion qui prêche la morale et la paix, et qui parle de devoirs et de vertus à toutes les conditions de la vie? Détruisez le culte évangélique, et il vous faudra dans chaque village une police, des prisons et des bourreaux.[11]

While sharing Chateaubriand's dislike of omnipresent policing, Courier clearly did not agree that Christian teaching was the only alternative. The question is revisited in Chapter 4.

The *biens nationaux* included the former owners' houses. Courier urged demolishing them and re-using the material for practical projects such as building bridges. But conservatives wanted the old estates, land and buildings alike, left intact or indeed restored to preserve historical memories. On this topic, a supposed neighbour says: 'Ils ne songent pas, les bonnes gens qui veulent maintenir toutes choses intactes, qu'à Dieu

10 Tulard, *Les Français sous Napoléon*, 109–19.

11 François-René de Chateaubriand, *Génie du christianisme*, 4 vols (Paris: Migneret, 1803), vol. 4, pp. 451–2. Cf. Emmanuel de Waresquiel, *Talleyrand: le prince immobile* (Paris: Fayard, 2006), 546.

seul appartient de créer; qu'on ne fait point sans défaire; que ne jamais détruire, c'est ne jamais renouveler' (*Lcens.* V, *OC*, 21; *Éc*, 193). Taking as his target one of the most eloquent conservatives, Félicité de Lamennais, the neighbour reduces this position to absurdity: 'Le jour de la création, quel bruit n'eût-il pas fait! Il eût crié: Mon Dieu, conservons le chaos' (ibid.).[12] Such hostility to material relics of the past probably owes its vigour partly to the stance of pre-Revolutionary nobles who had often argued that institutions and privileges which had lasted so long must be beneficial and need no change.[13] Ancestral homes, by their continued presence and the memories attached to them, might be taken to bolster such views. But the speaker maintains that these are memories of a loathsome past:

> Est-ce par les souvenirs que se recommandent ces châteaux et ces cloîtres gothiques ? Autour de nous, Chenonceaux, le Plessis-lèz-Tours, Blois, Amboise, Marmoutiers, que retracent-ils à l'esprit ? de honteuses débauches, d'infâmes trahisons, des assassinats, des massacres, des supplices, des tortures, d'exécrables forfaits, le luxe et la luxure, et la crasse ignorance des abbés et des moines, et, pis encore, l'hypocrisie. (*Lcens.* V *OC*, 20; *Éc*, 192)

Though this is evidently hyperbole, some of these places are indeed associated with terrible events: Blois with the murder of the Duc de Guise in 1588, for example, Amboise with the ferocious repression of a failed Huguenot plot in 1560. And the neighbour's contention is plausible: these monuments to shameful, multifarious degeneracy suggest that generations of former owners had done great evil and give no moral support to their current successors' demands for the restitution of the expropriated property.

However, Courier's inclination to demolish ancient properties for building materials makes experts uneasy. Crouzet refers to 'utilitarisme que l'on peut dire fanatique', Lautman notes that 'on a souvent reproché cet excès à Paul-Louis, voyant en lui une espèce de vandale'.[14] A connected

12 Lamennais had published an influential *Essai sur l'indifférence en matière de religion* (1817). Bertier, 310–12.

13 Baczko, Bronislaw, *Politiques de la Révolution française* (Paris: Gallimard (Folio histoire), 2008), 12.

14 Crouzet, 194, n. 2; Lautman, 180.

issue is obviously that of beauty versus utility, on which Courier's general views varied slightly. He wrote to his father Jean-Paul that at Sceaux he had seen 'de beaux jets d'eau, de belles statues et de beaux arbres bien taillés' but that 's'il y avait du froment ou des pommiers cela ne serait pas si beau, mais cela vaudrait mieux' (7 [1], 28 April 1787, *CG* I, 57). His stated preference for utility seems genuine, but our reading must be slightly cautious because he was only 15 and perhaps inclined to express views congenial to Jean-Paul. Thirty years later, Courier's 'neighbour' implies some appreciation of architecture in accepting that artistic worth might justify saving a few buildings, 'utiles aux arts comme modèles' (*Lcens*.V, *OC*, 20; *Éc*, 192). This concession, though lukewarm, suggests that Courier's preference for utility was not quite 'fanatique'. Regarding the historical character of old estates, the wish to eradicate memories of the aristocracy is understandable but apparently neglects the argument that some monuments belonged to the history of the whole nation and should be preserved for the nation. The historical value of artefacts from the *ancien régime* had indeed been recognized officially in France by about 1800.[15] Lautman seems, then, right to accept that Courier was guilty of some 'excès'.

The second chronic issue, the role of the Sainte Alliance, includes the possibility that it might remain in occupation, a topical eventuality after the murder of the duc de Berry. In general, national independence interests Courier less than personal freedom. But the two come together when loss of independence threatens individual freedoms, such as freedom of expression. The connection appears in *Lettre* X *au 'Censeur'*, inspired by parliamentary debates in March 1820 on press censorship. The letter includes an imaginary speech that Courier would have delivered if he had been a député. His real audience would have been the Allies and their reactionary French 'amis', who hope that the Alliance will restore the *ancien régime*. As the speech is essentially about foreign powers meddling in France, it begins and ends by warning the Allies against the advice of their 'amis' whose 'notes

15 The Musée des monuments français is a revealing case. This repository of sculpture and architectural remains was founded under the Revolution to provide models for artists and evidence for art historians, but by 1800 its general historical value was also recognized. See Francis Haskell, *History and Its Images* (New Haven: Yale University Press, revised edn, 1995), ch. 9.

secrètes' encourage reinvasion. Such clandestine letters did exist, the best known 'note secrète' having emanated in May 1818 from the ultra-royalist circles of Louis XVIII's brother, the duc d'Artois. That letter to the Allies, who still occupied France at the time but were conferring in Aachen on the country's future, allegedly warned them of a possible new Revolution, and urged them to guard against it by continuing the occupation. The exact tenor of the note was disputed, but it did seem to encourage foreign intervention in French affairs.[16] Fairly or unfairly, this is the 'note secrète' of which Courier's readers would probably have thought.

The 'notes secrètes' allegedly assure the Allies that they will meet scant resistance (*Lcens.* X, *OC*, 42–3; *Éc*, 216). But Courier asserts that they would be opposed by many, greeted by few. The few would include nobles, both pre-Revolutionary and Napoleonic: 'tout ce qui est issu de race, ou destiné à faire race, s'accommode sans peine avec vous' (*Lcens.* X, *OC*, 45; *Éc*, 219). The attitude attributed by Courier to the new nobles appears odd, for many had fought under Napoleon against powers now in the Alliance. His explanation is that, as a matter of fact, men who willingly risked their lives in war, now value honours and wealth more than they valued life itself: 'Aurions-nous vu [...] souvent le plus brave soldat être le plus lâche courtisan, s'il n'était vrai qu'on aime les biens et les honneurs plus que la vie?' (*LCens.* X, *OC*, 44; *Éc*, 218). The Church, too, would support the Allies, chiefly for material gain. Thus, nuns will beseech God to 'livrer à la fureur du glaive les ennemis de son saint nom, c'est-à-dire ceux qui refusent la dîme' (ibid.). Courier detests privileged individuals and groups willing to ally with foreign invaders, and it is noteworthy that his revulsion is general, not limited to these French cases. Twenty years before, a letter to Klewanski had reviled Italian collaborators, 'quelques grands seigneurs d'Italie [...] qui font, pour bien vivre avec les Français, des bassesses souvent inutiles' (43 [13], 8 January 1799, *CG* I, 103). Very importantly, then, his strictures on French supporters of the Allies are not merely nationalistic but seem to reflect his views about honour. In a country where personal honour was often envisaged as a particular attribute of the aristocracy, to

16 Waresquiel, *Talleyrand*, 529, Bertier, 151.

accuse noblemen of unbecoming behaviour, as Courier does, is particularly pointed. The subject is examined further in Chapter 3.

As for the many who would oppose the Alliance, their resilience has admittedly dwindled under Napoleon's authoritarian Empire (*LCens*. X, *OC*, 43; *Éc*, 217), but they will still resist. If the Allies meddle by influencing the government, they will be resisted in parliament for, despite the obstacles, opposition candidates continue to be elected: 'dès qu'il s'agit d'élire, les choix tombent sur des hommes [...] en voilà cent quinze de compte fait dans une seule chambre' (ibid.).[17] Against the now corrupted Napoleonic aristocracy of war heroes, Courier observes that 'celui qui meurt pour son pays fait moins que celui qui refuse de gouverner contre les lois. Or, de telles gens, nous en avons' (*LCens*. X, *OC*, 44; *Éc*, 218). This observation is central to Courier's thinking. For him legality is the cornerstone of good government and liberty. His wary attachment to the *Charte* reflects the same outlook. The *Pamphlet des pamphlets* (1824) was to laud the American people as 'le seul instruit de ce qu'il faut savoir pour n'obéir qu'aux lois' (*OC*, 217; *Éc*, 458).

If, moreover, the Allies meddle militarily, the parliamentary opposition could take up arms, and be followed by the people (*LCens*. X, *OC*, 44; *Éc*, 218). In terms that recall Letter *132* [37] from Calabria, Courier warns: 'Il y a peu de plaisir à conquérir des gens qui ne veulent pas être conquis, et nous en savons des nouvelles. Rien ne dégoûte de ce métier comme d'avoir affaire aux classes inférieures' (*LCens*. X, *OC*, 47; *Éc*, 220–1). Just as the French had suffered in Calabria from irregular resistance, so too will anyone invading France. From the military point of view, however, the cases differ: Courier attributed the French army's setbacks in Calabria partly to its own shortcomings, not wholly to the quality of the insurgency; but in France, he writes, even well-led regulars will struggle against irregular warfare (*LCens*. X, *OC*, 46; *Éc*, 220). The resistance that Courier expects in France would differ in its recruitment and motivation. Calabrians were sometimes criminal, their leadership was partly clerical, and religious zeal a

17 'Given the narrowness of the franchise and the control exercised by the government over elections, the strength achieved by the opposition in the parliaments of the Restoration is truly surprising' (Cobban, vol. 2, p. 78).

major motive. French resistance would rely on reputable individuals with military experience:

> Il n'est vilain qui n'en ait fait son apprentissage [...]. Georges le laboureur, André le vigneron, Pierre, Jacques le bonhomme, et Charles qui cultive ses trois cents arpents de terre, et le marchand, l'artisan, le juge, l'avocat, et notre digne vicaire, tous ont porté les armes; tous vous ont fait la guerre. (Ibid)

The leadership would not be clerical, and religion certainly not a motive. Courier jokes indeed that 'si vous venez les piller au nom de la très sainte et très indivisible Trinité, eux, au nom de leurs familles, de leurs champs, de leurs troupeaux, vous tireront des coups de fusil' (ibid.). Against the professed piety of the Sainte Alliance, the insurgents would be inspired by will to defend themselves and their possessions. Lucid self-interest, in short, would lead this socially mixed group to cooperate for mutual defence. In addition to their property, they would be defending their personal freedom: as freedom includes each man's being master in his own private sphere, repelling foreign interlopers is a very direct defence of individual liberty. Courier does not mention patriotism. No doubt it would have seemed needless and perhaps inconsistent to do so: needless, because he thought self-interest motive enough; inconsistent because of the non-partisan, objective view of foreign enemies which he showed towards the Calabrians in 1806.[18] Though no irregular resistance had occurred in 1814, Courier's threat remains credible in 1820.[19]

After the duc de Berry was killed, Louis's ministers sought to curtail press freedom. The *Charte* provided that 'Les Français ont le droit de publier et faire imprimer leurs opinions, en se conformant aux lois qui doivent réprimer les abus de cette liberté' (Art. 8). As the article allows legal sanctions against 'abus', restrictions can be constitutional. What the

18 However, Robert Gaschet, *Paul-Louis Courier et la Restauration* (Paris: Hachette, 1913), 103, refers to Courier's 'âpre patriotisme' (p. 103); Auerbach calls him 'ein ausgesprochener Nationalist' (p. 531).

19 In 1813, Wellington had anticipated such resistance in France 'where the whole population is armed and organised under persons [... who] must, the majority of them at least, have served somewhere'. Quoted in Charles Esdaile, *The Peninsular War* (London: Penguin Books, 2003), 456.

Charte implicitly excludes, however, is the general censorship introduced by the *loi d'exception contre la liberté de la presse*, (*loi du 30 mars 1820*). Courier raises the issue notably in the last two *Lettres au 'Censeur'*. *Lettre IX* offers a three-page fictional history of expression, starting from the inchoate utterances of primitive man. The text is systematically ironic, being attributed to an imagined historian whose perspective is broadly that of the royal court, the opposite of Courier's own. Letter VIII had already satirized the distribution of favours to courtiers, as 'prizes' for various categories of abject behaviour from lying and flattery to prostitution (*LCens.* VIII, *OC*, 32–3; *Éc*, 205–6). According to the pseudo-historian, such practices are threatened if any kind of expression is allowed, and he complains that rulers had failed to stifle prehistoric man's first mumblings:

> si on eût [...] mis au secret le premier qui s'avisa de dire *ba be bi bo bu*, le monde était sauvé [...] les pensions, les traitements, augmenteraient chaque année [...] Nymphes de l'Opéra vous auriez part encore à la mense abbatiale et au revenu des pauvres. (*LCens.* IX, *OC*, 35; *Éc*, 209)

The imaginary writer assumes that men naturally criticize rulers: 'Faute de mesures préventives [...] les hommes parlèrent, et tout aussitôt commencèrent à médire de l'autorité' (ibid.). With the inventions of writing, then of printing, the threat to governments grows (*OC*, 35–6; *Éc*, 209–10). The threat lies especially in the public's increased and increasing rationality, stimulated no doubt by the flow of information: apart from the higher nobility and the monks, 'tout le reste est perverti, tout le reste raisonne, ou bientôt raisonnera' and 'il n'y a plus moyen de gouverner' (*OC*, 36; *Éc*, 210). Here, reason is above all critical: 'que pourrait entreprendre la cour, qui ne fût contrôlé d'avance, examiné, jugé, critiqué, apprécié?' (ibid.) This ironic piece is interesting for two reasons. First, it is one of Courier's main applications of the liberal idea of human, intellectual progress; and he uses the idea in a strictly critical fashion. And secondly, more importantly, it conveys that governments are naturally corrupt, and that free speech is a major defence against corruption.

Lettre X is less whimsical and begins by accusing the parliamentary opposition of naïvety when debating the censorship bill. Constant had argued, for instance, that ministers themselves need information and so benefit from the news reported by a free press. Courier finds that this argument misses the essential truth about ministerial government: 'le point pour un ministre, c'est de rester ministre' (*LCens.* X, *OC*, 39; *Éc*, 213). As a minister's tenure depends on royal favour, not on events in the country, he needs to know 'non ce qui s'est fait à Lyon, mais ce qui s'est dit au lever, dont ne parlent pas les journaux' (ibid.). Besides, Courier claims, a minister should fear the spread of information. To keep his place, he must appear a zealous guardian of the king, and so he must thwart plots. If there are no plots, ministers invent them: 'Les faire naître, les étouffer, charger la mine, l'éventer, c'est le grand art du ministère' (*OC*, 39; *Éc*, 214). This view of underhand ministerial activity seems exaggerated, but plainly press freedom would hamper any such oppressive manœuvres:

> Les journaux [...] apprennent au public ce que les ministres font, chose fort intéressante, ou ce qu'ils veulent faire, encore meilleur à savoir [...] Le secret, en un mot, est l'âme de la politique, et la publicité n'est bonne que pour le public. (*OC*, 40; *Éc*, 214)[20]

That is Courier's version of the idea that press freedom protects individual freedom. In fact, that view was held quite widely and, despite his strictures on Constant's performance, Courier's view converges with some of Constant's arguments. Thus, Constant decries the censorship bill designed to

> enchaîner la liberté de la presse et tuer la publicité, seule garantie réelle des citoyens [...] Les ministres espèrent trouver dans cette mesure un moyen d'empêcher que, s'ils abusent du pouvoir discrétionnaire [...] pour incarcérer quiconque leur déplaira, cet abus ne soit dénoncé.[21]

Constant and Courier agree that *publicité* is crucial to freedom. However, there is a marked difference in tone and in focus. Constant thinks

20 Some conspiracies were real, not ministerial fictions (Bertier, 180–3).

21 Constant, *Discours à la Chambre des députés*, 2 vols (Paris: Dupont, 1828), vol. 1, pp. 232–3; Id. *De la liberté des brochures*, in *Œuvres*, 1240; Arthur Ghinns, 'Benjamin Constant and Public Opinion', *History of Political Thought*, 40/3 (2019), 484–514.

primarily of protecting individual subjects. Courier shares this concern, but he highlights the motive which he takes to underlie arbitrary arrests and punishments, namely individual ministers' personal ambitions. The parliamentary opposition, he felt, had paid insufficient heed to these moral aspects of the situation.

The *Lettres particulières* relate broadly to the election of November 1820 and more specifically to the loyalty of the forces. The government needed troops to keep order as, for example, in Paris during riots against the electoral bill in early June 1820.[22] But the forces' loyalties were divided, as witnessed in the account in the first *Lettre particulière* of events in October 1820. When Constant visited Saumur for his election campaign, his supporters were attacked by some aristocratic regular officers from the garrison, who were themselves assailed in turn by the garde nationale (*Lpart* (1), *OC*, 58; *Éc*, 239). The garde was a militia created to support the civil power and, because its units might follow local political tendencies, their allegiance to the central government was uncertain.[23] Within the regular army, meanwhile, non-commissioned officers or officers who had risen from the ranks were at odds with aristocratic officers: 'les bas officiers ou ceux qui l'ont été, qu'on appelle à présent officiers de fortune, s'accommodent mal avec les officiers de naissance' (*Lpart* (1), *OC*, 56; *Éc*, 236). According to the *Lettre*, tensions arise partly from the NCOs' revolutionary tradition (ibid.). The point is dramatized in a dialogue between an aristocratic lieutenant and his sergeant during the Saumur episode. At first, when the lieutenant calls Constant 'un coquin, un homme de la révolution' (*Lpart* (1), *OC*, 56; *Éc*, 237), the sergeant is – or pretends to be – willing to attack him. However, in the subsequent exchanges, the sergeant's questions and the lieutenant's answers bring out a radical divergence of interests. For the sergeant, the Revolution was good, because it enabled all to seek promotion and abolished cruel punishments: 'la révolution [...] nous fit des officiers, ôta les coups de bâton' (*Lpart* (1), *OC*, 57; *Éc*, 237). For the lieutenant, these changes were aberrant and will soon be rectified, perhaps with Allied help, for 'Martin bâton commande les troupes de la Sainte-Alliance' (*Lpart* (1),

22 Bertier, 169–70.
23 Price, 204–5; Bertier, 152.

OC, 57; *Éc*, 238). The division is irreconcilable. The lieutenant believes in an immovable social hierarchy: 'il faut que chacun demeure dans sa classe; autrement ce serait un désordre, une cohue' (*Lpart* (1), *OC*, 57–8; *Éc*, 238). The sergeant fears regression to the situation as it was under the *ancien régime* and declines to follow the officer against Constant (*Lpart* (1), *OC*, 58; *Éc*, 238). Because the recently departed ministre de la Guerre, Gouvion Saint-Cyr, had legislated to protect promotion from the ranks, the matter was topical and doubtless led to conflicts such as that dramatized here.[24] At all events, an army so divided is unreliable. The second *Lettre particulière*, after a comical account of voting in the election, returns to the army. In a dialogue between Courier's persona, bonhomme Paul, and a soldier who had been one of Paul's neighbours, two points emerge. First, the government does not intend the army to defend the country against foreign powers. The soldier thinks his training futile: 'Pour quelle guerre ? On s'y prend de manière à n'avoir jamais de querelle avec les puissances étrangères' (*Lpart* (2), *OC*, 69; *Éc*, 249). The army's only remaining function is to quell unrest in the civilian population. This raises the second point, the rankers' reluctance to use their arms against their own people. The soldier protests indignantly: 'Moi, vous sabrer, bonhomme! Quiconque vous l'a dit est un …' (*Lpart* (2), *OC*, 69; *Éc*, 250). While showing interest in the well-being of ordinary soldiers, Courier's main message here is that the government cannot rely on the garde nationale or even the regular army as repressive forces.

The early political pamphlets exemplify several notable expressive strategies including Courier's adoption of a persona as speaker or writer. In the *Pétition*, he places his address to the legislators in the mouth of an unnamed inhabitant of Luynes. This resident claims from the outset that he disapproves of some of his neighbours' behaviour: he says of Fouquet, who failed to make way for a funeral and swore at the priest, 'Il fit mal; je le blâme, et le blâmai dès lors' (*OC*, 3; *Éc*, 124). Having asserted his respectable values, he goes on to present himself as a mere villager, simple like the others: he writes, for instance, about the arrest of the alleged 'bonapartistes', that 'nous autres, gens de village, nous ne sommes pas accoutumés à ces coups d'État'

24 Bertier, 147–8; *Éc*, 241, n. 3.

(*OC*, 5; *Éc*, 125). But he speaks visibly with tongue-in-cheek, for he displays literacy and acquaintance with political questions: he quotes, for example, from Chateaubriand's recent, prohibited work, *De la monarchie selon la Charte* (*OC*, 4; *Éc*, 125) and his allusion to the Ligue (*OC*, 9; *Éc*, 130) may echo discreetly La Fontaine's fable *La chauve-souris et les deux belettes.*[25] He is also capable of rhetorical flourishes, as when he exclaims: 'Justice, équité, providence! vains mots dont on nous abuse!' (*OC*, 6; *Éc*, 127). In fact, two imaginary figures, that is, two personae of Courier overlap here: a first persona, the simple villager; and a second persona, the educated man pretending to be a simple villager. The legislators are thus invited to bear in mind his simplicity, which is typical of the other villagers, but also to see him as a cultivated petitioner urging them to take the case seriously.

A different persona of Courier appears in *Lettre X au 'Censeur'*, where he refers to himself under his own identity, but with some imaginary traits added. In describing the speech that he would have delivered in the censorship debate, had he been a député, he claims that the opposition had been too polite and hence bound to fail.[26] As no government listens unless shocked, he recommends apostrophe, a 'figure de rhétorique par laquelle un orateur interpelle tout à coup une personne'.[27] The opposition had avoided such abruptness 'car l'apostrophe n'est pas polie' (*OC*, 41; *Éc*, 215). Courier also calls apostrophe 'une figure au moyen de laquelle on a trouvé le secret de parler aux gens qui ne sont pas là' (ibid.). If, as he implies, the Sainte Alliance has dictated the bill, his persona must indeed defy 'gens qui ne sont pas là'. To illustrate his imagined liking for apostrophe, he writes: 'je ne parle guère autrement, je ne dis jamais: *Nicole, apporte-moi mes pantoufles, mais je dis: O mes pantoufles: et toi, Nicole, et toi !* ...' (*OC*, 42; *Éc*, 216). The allusion is to a familiar scene in Molière's *Bourgeois gentilhomme*, in which M. Jourdain learns, to his amazement, that he is speaking in prose when he says: 'Nicole, apportez-moi mes pantoufles' (Act II, scene 4). Courier apostrophizes the ministers of Britain, Austria, and Prussia with dismissive imperatives: '*Mylord Castlereagh*, mêlez-vous de vos affaires; pour Dieu,

25 'Le Sage dit, selon les gens:/ Vive le Roi, vive la Ligue' (*Fables*, II, 5, ll. 33–4).

26 The debate was actually heated (Gaschet, 97–9).

27 *Petit Robert*, s.v. 'apostrophe'.

Herr Metternich, laissez-nous en repos; et vous, *Mein lieber Hardenberg*, songez à bien cuire vos *sauerkraut*' (ibid.). Sending Hardenberg to cook a humble *choucroute* assimilates him additionally to a servant like Nicole. Perhaps more importantly, in alluding to M. Jourdain, Courier also creates a comic aura around himself and the ministers, combining self-mockery with derision of his target. And he adds, with a comic show of caution and modesty: 'Ou je me trompe, ou cette tournure eût fait effet sur l'assemblée, eût éveillé son attention' (ibid.). Clearly, the persona in the *Pétition* is unlike his comically stentorian counterpart in *Lettre X*. Courier personae are not simply one habitual, invariable *alter ego* of the author, but a range of characters who differ widely from one text to another.

The *Lettres au 'Censeur'* also deploy personae completely distinct from the writer, such as the pseudo-historian in *Lettre IX*. *Lettre V* includes both a Courier persona and, the figure of a supposed neighbour (*OC*, 18; *Éc*, 190). The 'neighbour' looks like a spokesman for Courier: in praising the *bandes noires* and decrying the shameful memories attached to ancient buildings (*OC*, 18–20; *Éc*, 190–2), he anticipates thoughts that Courier expresses in his own name in the *Simple Discours* (*OC*, 86; *Éc*, 274). But in *Lettre V* the persona of Courier himself ostensibly disagrees with his neighbour and claims to prefer the old days, when the poor lived from charity, not work: 'Chaque jour la charité s'éteint, depuis qu'on songe à travailler, et se perdra enfin, si la Sainte-Alliance n'y met ordre' (*OC*, 22; *Éc*, 193). This is a simple case of irony: in *Lettre V*, the main sense is of course that it is perverse to promote charity over work.

Irony is indeed a second major feature of expression in the early political pamphlets. *Lettre V* is one of several advancing ironically views that Courier rejects elsewhere: for example, *Lettre IV* lauds the prosecutors (*OC*, 17; *Éc*, 189), *Lettre VI* the return of land from industrious peasants to the former owners, idle aristocrats and churchmen (*OC*, 24; *Éc*, 196). It is particularly significant in the *Pétition aux deux Chambres.*[28] One example is the contrast between the treatment of Fouquet,[29] and Georges Mauclair,

28 Jean-Claude Baudroux, 'Essai de définition de l'ironie chez Paul-Louis Courier', *Cahiers Paul-Louis Courier*, 3/1–2 (1990), 17–22.

29 François Fouquet was not involved. Courier confuses him with Jean Fouquet, who was the real accused (Jean-Pierre Lautman, 'De "L'infâme affaire" à la Pétition aux deux Chambres', *Cahiers Paul-Louis Courier*, V/3 (2017), 65–116 (pp. 81–3)).

on the one hand, and that of a third, unnamed villager. After reading about Fouquet's imprisonment, we learn that: 'On arrêta vers le même temps, et pour une cause aussi grave, Georges Mauclair', who had allegedly 'mal parlé [...] du gouvernement' (*OC*, 4; *Éc*, 125). Here, in its context, 'aussi grave' means literally 'equally serious', while implying 'equally frivolous'. Mauclair had presumably criticized the government, but the speaker professes to understand that he had spoken ineptly. The villagers know little of politics and, 'si Georges Mauclair en a voulu parler, je ne m'étonne pas qu'il en ait mal parlé; mais je m'étonne qu'on l'ait mis en prison pour cela. C'est être un peu sévère, ce me semble' (ibid.). The understatement, 'un peu sévère' conveys ironically its opposite: 'très sévère'. The speaker then cites the third case: 'J'approuve bien plus l'indulgence qu'on a eue pour un autre', that is, a villager whose flagrantly Bonapartist utterances were ignored. Here, the approval of 'indulgence' may perhaps be taken literally, but the predominant sense is clearly that the speaker deplores the authorities' inconsistency. In the *Pétition*, then, irony is less systematic and less implacable than in the *Lettre IX*, but it is apt. It is thinly disguised and suits the speaker's two-sided persona: not being too subtle, it befits the simple villager; but, being irony, it also befits the educated man who lets his audience see that he is speaking tongue-in-cheek.

Are these two sets of *Lettres* epistolary in manner? Courier's real letters are short, rarely over two pages in Allem's edition. The *Lettres au 'Censeur'* are slightly longer, I–IX averaging about three pages. The 10-page *Lettre X* is not very epistolary, since it begins as a letter to the editor, but turns into a speech to the legislature. The *Lettres particulières* occupy six and a half and ten pages, respectively, and in length are nearer to Courier's other pamphlets: for example, the *Pétition aux deux Chambres* runs to seven and a half pages, the *Simple Discours* over fifteen. In length, then, it is the *Lettres au 'Censeur'* which are more akin to Courier's personal letters than to the other pamphlets. Such concision gives certain *Lettres* particular impact: for example, the first, which conveys in under two pages the progress of the peasants' lot since Louis XIV, or the fourth, which ridicules the royal prosecutors in just over two pages.

Courier's letters, especially to fellow soldiers, can be informal or jocularly insulting, as in the opening: 'Vous êtes de mauvais plaisants, et votre conte ne vaut rien' (124 [35], 13 December 1805, *CG* I, 211). Courier can be similarly blunt in professing to correct the editor of the *Censeur*. The first *Lettre* begins: 'Vous vous trompez, monsieur, vous avez tort de croire que mon placet imprimé [...] n'a produit nul effet' (*OC*, 10; *Éc*, 182). Later in the *Lettre*, the writer again engages briskly with the editor:

> Vous nous plaignez beaucoup, nous autres paysans, et vous avez raison [...] Mais songez donc, monsieur, qu'autrefois on nous tuait pour *cinq sous parisis* [...] Vous paraît-il, monsieur, que nous ayons peu gagné en cinq ou six cents ans? (*OC*, 11; *Éc*, 182–3)

There are also structural similarities. Some of Courier's personal letters are loosely constructed, as he digresses to repair oversights or possible omissions. Thus, he interrupts news of fighting to ask for the return of a bridle: 'En parenthèse de peur que je ne l'oublie; renvoie-moi [...] ma bride à la housarde' (147 [49], 1806, *CG* I, 266). In some *Lettres*, too, he rectifies in passing his own (supposed) oversights. Late in *Lettre IV*, for example, he interjects: 'Mais je me suis trompé, monsieur, je m'en aperçois; ce n'est pas là toute la lettre du procureur du roi' (*OC*, 17; *Éc*, 188). This 'correction' highlights the prosecutors' care with polite formulae and, by contrast, their disdain for the forms of judicial process and for the substance of justice. Clearly, the loose, seemingly spontaneous manner enhances the impact of some *Lettres au 'Censeur'*.

While the relative length of the *Lettres particulières* foreshadows later pamphlets, they are apparently addressed to individual correspondents, and the seemingly disconnected snippets of news which they contain are also characteristic of many real, personal letters. Both *Lettres* are also allusive, suggesting complicity between Courier and his imaginary correspondent. Complicity is typical of real letters but may create obscurity here. Thus the first *Lettre* opens with a paragraph purporting to answer some points which Courier's imagined correspondent has made about new leases:

> Nos métayers sont des fripons qui vendent la poule au renard; leurs valets me semblent comme à vous les plus méchants drôles qu'on ait vus depuis bien du temps. Ils ont mis le feu aux granges, et maintenant, pour l'éteindre, ils appellent les voleurs. [...] nous ferons un autre bail avec d'autres fripons; mais il faudra compter, il faudra faire une part à cette valetaille, puisqu'on ne peut s'en passer. (*OC*, 55; *Éc*, 235)

Dated 18 October, just before the elections of November 1820, the *Lettre* probably refers to the misdeeds of the outgoing government and its reliance on the 'voleurs' of the Sainte Alliance. If this interpretation is reasonable, the underlying idea is of course that the ministers have a subordinate position, they are *métayers*, tenants of the electorate. Beyond that, the allegory has the advantage of accusing the king's ministers of corruption – but only by implication. That was perhaps prudent in repressive times, but the possible lack of clarity weakens the controversialist's message.

In summary, these first pamphlets introduce major themes in Courier's writing, such as personal freedom, especially from local tyrants, smallholders' property rights and rejection of foreign interference, particularly in relation to freedom of speech. They also imply Courier's independence from the parliamentary liberals, of whom he is sharply critical. In form, these pamphlets already display highly developed use of ironies and of personae, and of subsidiary features such as literary allusion and dialogue.

CHAPTER 3

Pamphlets, 1821–1822: Chambord and the Secular Establishment

Events after Berry's murder inspired one of Courier's main pamphlets, the *Simple Discours*, with three companion texts, *Aux âmes dévotes de la paroisse de Véretz*, the *Procès de Paul-Louis Courier*, and part of the first *Réponse aux anonymes*. The birth in September 1820 of Berry's posthumous son Henri caused initial enthusiasm: Louis XVIII made him duc de Bordeaux, and a public subscription was launched to buy him the estate of Chambord. For advocates of this purchase, it both demonstrated popular joy, and also protected the estate's integrity. Napoleon had given Chambord and a pension to Marshal Berthier but, when he died in 1815, his pension stopped and his widow could not maintain the property.[1] Being hard to sell as one lot, it seemed likely to be dismembered and sold piecemeal, but purchase for Henri removed that prospect. Courier's local council, Véretz, considered subscribing and, though it decided against, the debate gave him a chance to object in his *Simple Discours*. For this pamphlet he was prosecuted, which directly inspired two more texts: *Aux âmes dévotes*, published before the trial, and the *Procès de Paul-Louis Courier*, published after. The planned purchase had raised two questions: whether the gift was desirable and, if so, who should pay for it. When Courier finished his *Discours*, the sale had been completed, and the subscription seemed fully launched.[2]

1 Gaschet, 113, Lautman, 194–6.

2 *OC*, 942, n. 1; *Éc*, 256. But Jean-Pierre Lautman argues that the projected purchase could still have been stopped when the pamphlet was published ('Le *Simple Discours*, réplique à la normalisation des esprits', *Cahiers Paul-Louis Courier*, 5/8 (2022), 53–108 (p. 105)). Writing to his wife, Courier suggests that the authorities are hesitating over the project (680 [202], April 1821, *CG* III, 271).

However, regarding payment, Courier declares that the parish of Véretz should not contribute, because it will have no money to spare until all its debts have been paid, its roads and its church repaired, and all its paupers relieved (*OC*, 72; *Éc*, 261). As these obligations are endless, diverting money to the Chambord subscription is unjustified, and will simply increase the hardship of ordinary people.

But the question which Courier highlights is the first, whether the gift is desirable. He answers in the negative, arguing that the gift harms both the Duke himself and the residents of Chambord. The Duke will suffer, as future monarch, because the subscription will alienate the people: 'Ce qu'il lui faut pour régner, ce ne sont pas des châteaux, c'est notre affection [...] Voilà le bien dont il a besoin et qu'il ne peut avoir en même temps que notre argent' (*OC*, 73; *Éc*, 262). The risks to the future king, however, go farther, as shown by Courier's criticism of the upbringing of French kings, and of French royal courts in general. He contends that most French kings have been isolated from their people by selfish courtiers. Typically, the latter now want Chambord, 'pour en être, l'un gouverneur, l'autre concierge, bien gagés, bien logés, bien nourris' (ibid.). Such claims recall traditional criticisms that courtiers interpose between the king and his people, or between the king and reality, and so lead him into dreadful mistakes. These strictures appear in early writers whom Courier knew, such as Commynes and Rabelais.[3] But Courier's criticism is topical because of its positive counterpart, his praise of the education currently being given at the Lycée Henri IV to the duc de Chartres. The pupil, the eldest son of Louis-Philippe, Duc d'Orléans, is the first prince to receive a school education rather than wholly private tuition (*OC*, 76; *Éc*, 265). According to Courier, attending school will familiarize him with the people, and if earlier princes had benefited from such familiarity, it would have spared kings and subjects alike some bloody episodes: 'Jamais de Dragonnades ni de Saint-Barthélemy, quand les rois, élevés au milieu de leur peuple, parleront

3 Philippe de Commynes, *Mémoires* in *Historiens et chroniqueurs du moyen âge*, ed. Albert Pauphilet and Edmond Pognon (Paris: Gallimard (Pléiade, 1952), Livre V, ch. 19, p. 1226; François Rabelais, *Gargantua*, in *Œuvres complètes*, ed. Mireille Huchon (Paris: Gallimard (Pléiade), 1994), ch. 33, p. 91.

la même langue, s'entendront avec eux sans truchement ni intermédiaire' (*OC*, 77; *Éc*, 266). At the Lycée Henri IV the young Duke did not meet the 'peuple' in Courier's usual sense (peasant farmers), but he almost certainly encountered progressive currents of thought. Louis-Philippe's choice of education provoked conflict between him and Louis XVIII, who feared that the young Duke might absorb politically dangerous ideas.[4] But other tensions underlay this disagreement. The Duc d'Orléans was head of the junior branch of the royal family and the Bourbons suspected that he had designs on the throne. Clearly, the Duc de Chartres could become king only if the Orléans replaced the Bourbons, and Courier's passage on the schoolboy prince could thus be taken to advocate such dynastic change.

While regretting that the court, whatever its location, will isolate the future king from his subjects, Courier also deplores the generally immoral behaviour of courtiers and the old aristocracy. *Lettre VIII au 'Censeur'* had already claimed that debased seekers after advancement fill the court. The *Discours* develops this claim, with two changes of emphasis. The first concerns responsibility for courtiers' abjection. The *Lettre* had caricatured a court where official prizes were offered for various vices as if the King had actively corrupted his courtiers. In the *Discours*, however, the courtiers themselves besiege the King in their quest for gain, and he is thus no longer accused of promoting wrongdoing. The second change is the added emphasis on the role of women. Some of the imagined prizes in *Lettre VIII* reward 'l'adultère et la prostitution, les plus enviés de tous, dont un seul fait souvent la grandeur d'une famille' (*OC*, 33; *Éc*, 205–6). The *Discours* goes farther and asserts categorically: 'il n'y a pas en France une seule famille noble […] d'antique origine, qui ne doive sa fortune aux femmes' (*OC*, 83; *Éc*, 271). Courier adds that the ascent of old noble families may appear due to 'le pillage, les concussions, l'assassinat, les proscriptions et surtout les confiscations' (ibid.), but he holds that, fundamentally, 'aucun de ces moyens n'eût pu être mis en œuvre sans la faveur d'un grand, obtenue par quelque femme' (ibid.). Prostitution, as the *Discours* repeats bluntly, was a necessary condition for these families to rise. This is an exaggeration, and

4 Arnaud Teyssier, *Louis-Philippe: Le dernier roi des Français* (Paris: Perrin, 2010), 109–12; Price, 99–100.

even the *Discours* concedes that some noblemen earn rewards by public service: in the previous century, for instance, Chambord 'fut au comte de Saxe le prix d'une victoire qui sauva la France à Fontenoi' (*OC*, 75; *Éc*, 263–4). However, the example is marginal for, as later indicated in the *Livret*, the count was not French, but the illegitimate son of a German nobleman (*OC*, 174; *Éc*, 409).

These strictures on courtiers' immorality in the *Discours* particularly convey a fear that the example of the Court would corrupt the local peasants. For Courier, their calling is work, which both earns income and promotes morality: as we know, *Lettre V au 'Censeur'* affirms that 'tout vice vient d'oisiveté' (*OC*, 19; *Éc*, 191). The *Discours* warns Courier's neighbours accordingly against the specious example of the court: having seen 'tous les honnêtes gens abhorrer le travail [...] vous renierez la terre votre mère, et l'abandonnerez' (*OC*, 81; *Éc*, 270). The impact of the court on the young will be especially damaging. If fathers persist in farming, 'vos fils vous abandonneront, s'en iront valets de valets à la cour' (ibid.). The example of the court will also foster licence, even in the peasants' own homes: 'vos filles, pour avoir seulement ouï parler de ce qui s'y passe, n'en vaudront guère mieux au logis' (ibid.). The *Discours* also emphasizes that, for the peasant, work promotes self-respect. Hence the warning that the self-abasement of courtiers exemplifies the contrary: 'Mendier n'est pas honte à la cour: c'est toute la vie du courtisan' (*OC*, 80; *Éc*, 269). The emphasis on the dignity of the humble is particularly important because it reverses the stereotype that the nobleman has a sense of his own dignity, of his own 'honneur', which by implication the peasant lacks. Chateaubriand, for instance, attributes to his father 'les qualités du gentilhomme, le courage, la probité, l'honneur'.[5] Here, it is obviously the mendicant noble who lacks self-respect, and the peasant who has self-respect because he lives off his own work.

The same passage also illuminates Courier's wider views about morality, especially peasant morality. Moral rigour, in contrast with the raffishness of some of his letters from Italy (e.g. 124 [35], 147 [49]) is already visible in

5 Jean-Claude Berchet, ed., *Mémoires de ma vie* in *Mémoires d'outre-tombe*, 4 vols (Paris: Garnier (Livre de Poche), 2001–2), vol. 1, p. 68. Cf. Arlette Jouanna, 'Honneur, Honneurs', *Dictionnaire de l'Ancien Régime*, 640–1.

the *Lettres au 'Censeur'*. In the *Discours*, on the courtiers' allegedly rampant promiscuity, he says to his imaginary peasant audience:

> Une telle vie, mes amis, vous paraît impossible à croire. [...] Vos maisons périraient, dites-vous, si les choses s'y passaient ainsi. Je le crois. Chez vous on vit de travail, d'économie [...] Chez vous, l'industrie du mari amène tous les biens à la maison, où la femme dispose, ordonne, règle chaque chose. (*OC*, 82–3; *Éc*, 271)

Courier's concern for sexual morality arises from considerations of domestic order; sexual morality is crucial for the well-being of the family, and thence, no doubt for the well-being of society. Fundamentally, his new moral rigour is based on utility, and not on religious or philosophical imperatives. Given such views, it is logical for him to fear that the court will be doubly pernicious, by discouraging work and encouraging licence. On the other hand, in condemning so vigorously the behaviour of aristocrats and courtiers of whatever social origins, he also implies that his faith in the moral rectitude of the 'peuple' is not unlimited. Indeed, he seems convinced that physical distance best preserves the peasants from courtly influence, and that a nearby court will inevitably corrupt most of them. Courier's emphasis on the value of morality in these passages is distinctive, and not characteristic of liberal thinking at the time.

A different matter, with both practical and symbolic importance, is the likely return of game animals to amuse the court. On the practical impact of damage to crops caused by game and hunters, the text quotes a supposed resident of Chambord, who recalls that 'Paris fut bloqué huit cents ans par les bêtes fauves, et sa banlieue [...] ne produisait pas de quoi nourrir les gardes de chasse' (*OC*, 85; *Éc*, 273). The symbolic importance of hunting is that, in some forms, it was a distinctive privilege of nobility and crown, and the concurrent return of *émigrés* and game marks a stage in political reaction. The same character says that the Revolution afforded some respite, but then 'le héros parut, et fit venir d'Allemagne des parents ou des alliés de nos ennemis morts dans la campagne de quatre-vingt-neuf. Vingt couples de cerfs arrivèrent, destinés à repeupler les bois, et ravager les champs pour le plaisir d'un homme' (ibid.). The 'héros' is Bonaparte who as Consul welcomed back *émigré* nobles and here is accused succinctly of undermining the Revolution and its benefits for the peasantry.[6]

While opposing the purchase of the estate for the Duc de Bordeaux, Courier also gives his own opinion about its future. Before the subscription, Chambord had seemed likely to fall to the so-called *bande noire*, the pejorative name applied to businessmen who bought former noble or ecclesiastical properties and sold them off profitably in small lots. For Courier, whose *Lettres au 'Censeur'* had lauded these businessmen, this solution was incomparably preferable. In the *Discours*, after lamenting the ravages of hunting, his imagined resident prays for the *bande noire* to buy Chambord (ibid.), and advises selling Chambord's 'douze mille arpents de terre' (ibid.) to 'trois ou quatre mille familles'.[7] Amid further praise of smallholding Courier, agreeing with his supposed resident, jests that the *bande noire* helps fulfil the word of God: 'Dieu dit: Croissez, multipliez, remplissez la terre, c'est-à-dire, cultivez-la bien; car, sans cela, comment peupler? et la partagez; sans cela, comment cultiver?' (*OC*, 86; *Éc*, 274).

The pamphlet caused a stir, as Courier reports in two letters to his wife: 'Mon Ch … rd a un grand succès, il s'en vend beaucoup' (683 [203], 1 May 1821, *CG* III, 275); 'Ma brochure a un succès fou [...] c'est de l'admiration, de l'enthousiasme, etc.' (690 [204], June 1821, *CG* III, 281). But the authorities were neither admiring nor enthusiastic, and prosecuted the writer. He initially risked twelve years' imprisonment on three charges: 'd'avoir offensé la morale publique [...] d'avoir en même temps offensé la personne du roi, et [...] provoqué à offenser ladite personne' (*Procès*, *OC*, 91; *Éc*, 285). With his trial pending, he published *Aux âmes dévotes*, which defiantly summarizes the claims of the *Discours* and mocks the hostility that it had produced. Compared with the *Discours*, this piece accentuates the distinction between king and courtiers, saying, for example, 'que les princes sont bons [...] et bien intentionnés; mais qu'ils vivent entourés d'une mauvaise valetaille qui les sépare de nous' (*Âmes*, *OC*, 88; *Éc*, 282). The new pamphlet also claims that the prosecution is a charade

6 Philippe Salvadori, 'Chasse', *Dictionnaire de l'Ancien Régime*, 250–1.

7 Courier, *Œuvres complètes*, ed. Armand Carrel, 4 vols (Paris: Paulin & Perrotin, 1834), vol. 1, p. 194. Allem and Crouzet give 'trois ou quatre familles' (*OC*, 85; *Éc*, 273).

to protect, not the 'personne du roi', but the illicit interests of the privileged. Thus, Paul-Louis bestows a special role on the prosecutors, whom he calls 'les syndics du corps de la flagornerie' (*OC*, 89–90; *Éc*, 282–3). In this capacity, they prosecute him 'comme ayant *offensé la morale publique*, en racontant ce qui se passe chez eux, et *la personne du roi* dans celle des courtisans' (*OC*, 90; *Éc*, 283). The *Discours* had hinted that partisan judges connived to protect courtiers' interests (*OC*, 80; *Éc*, 268), but the perspective on partisan prosecutors is new. Hitherto, Courier had seen them as tools of tyrannical executive power, here they are servants of a sordidly privileged group.

Aux âmes dévotes drastically condenses the *Discours*: for example, most of the earlier pamphlet's content is crystallized in the statement that 'eux, gens de cour, sont à nous autres, gens de travail et d'industrie, cause de tous maux' (*Âmes*, *OC*, 88; *Éc*, 281). Those unfamiliar with the *Discours* might find *Aux âmes dévotes* puzzling and gratuitous, but for those who know the *Discours*, the laconic statements to which this latter is reduced have great impact. The reduction also has a more subtle satirical effect. The complainants' wrath centres on some eleven 'propositions scandaleuses, impies et révolutionnaires' which they have extracted from the *Discours* (*Âmes*, *OC*, 89; *Éc*, 282); the quotation about 'gens de cour', above, is the first of the eleven. What Paul-Louis calls 'propositions …' are actually his own summary of the *Discours*. But, by asserting that his opponents have isolated and damned them, he attributes to his adversaries a method used in doctrinal controversies of the past. Medieval and Reformation theologians, seeking to prove a text heretical, distilled its content into brief statements ('conclusions'), which they then damned in fairly standardized terms. The phrase 'scandaleuses, impies et révolutionnaires' recalls a sixteenth-century formula used by the Sorbonne: 'conclusionem esse scandalosam, offensivam piarum aurium, haeresim sapientem' [scandalous, offensive to pious ears and smelling of heresy].[8] The satirical parallel implies that Paul-Louis's antagonists are intolerant hypocrites, pretending to defend morality and monarchy, while simply protecting vested interests.

8 Quoted in Rabelais, *Œuvres complètes*, 1083, n. 13. Cf. *Gargantua*, ch. 7, p. 23.

As a mocking reaffirmation of the *Discours*, *Aux âmes dévotes* was a challenge to the prosecutors. On the advice of his lawyer Me Berville, Courier initially withheld the text, but he later published it because counterfeit copies were circulating.[9] If they were aware of the new pamphlet, the authorities seem to have been unmoved, for the most serious charges against Courier were later dropped, leaving only that of 'outrage à la morale publique'. He was convicted on 29 August 1821 and received a relatively lenient sentence of two months in prison and a fine of 300 francs. He again reacted defiantly, this time by giving his version of the trial in the *Procès de Paul-Louis Courier*. Before studying this text, however, we must recall what was understood by 'outrage à la morale publique'. The relevant statute was the *loi du 17 mai 1819* on the freedom of the press.[10] Under section 8, 'Tout outrage à la morale publique et religieuse ou aux bonnes mœurs [...] sera puni d'un emprisonnement d'un mois à un an, et d'une amende de 16 francs à 500 francs'. 'Outrage ... aux bonnes mœurs' concerned obscenity, but what of 'outrage à la morale publique'? In parliamentary debate, critics objected that too many interpretations were possible.[11] Defending the bill, the Garde des Sceaux, Hercule de Serre, stated that 'morale publique' denoted innate, universal rules:

> La morale publique est celle que la conscience et la raison révèlent à tous les peuples comme à tous les hommes, parce que tous l'ont reçue de leur divin auteur, en même tems que l'existence; morale contemporaine de toutes les sociétés.

These were, he asserted, beliefs and values essential to the very survival of any society:

> les notions d'un Dieu vengeur et rémunérateur du juste et de l'injuste, du vice et de la vertu, [...] le respect pour les auteurs de ses jours et pour la vieillesse, [...] la tendresse pour les enfants, [...] le dévouement au prince, [...] l'amour de la patrie, [...] toutes les vertus enfin [...] sans lesquelles tous les peuples sont condamnés à périr.

9 Letter to Me Berville, 691 [208], 3 July 1821, *CG* III, 282.

10 André Laingui, 'Les Magistrats du XIXe siècle juges des écrivains de leur temps', *Cahiers de l'Association internationale des études françaises*, 44 (1992), 221–41 (p. 224).

11 *Moniteur Universel*, 15 April 1819, p. 5.

That was what we might call a 'universalist' view. But he modified it by adding that 'la morale publique':

> c'est pour les nations le premier des patrimoines, le plus précieux des trésors; il s'enrichit de tous les actes de vertu; de tous les dévouemens, de tous les sacrifices ... La France est riche déjà de ce patrimoine.[12]

This further gloss extends the scope of the legislation to protect the historical record of 'actes de vertu ... dévouemens ... sacrifices', perhaps because these could inspire public-spirited actions. This additional explanation gives the notion of 'morale publique' a 'national' content, specific to each nation, as distinguished from the universal principles outlined initially. De Serre's remarks were not themselves the law, but they suggest a climate of opinion in which the law was liable to be interpreted in a 'national' spirit.

The climate mattered particularly because such cases were tried by jury. Jurors were assumed to have a grasp of the principles extolled by de Serre and also to represent public opinion. The idea thus prevailed that jurors needed no definitions in article 8 of the statute, but could decide for themselves what would constitute an affront to 'morale publique', and whether a particular publication was such an affront. A committee of the Chambre des Pairs endorsed this open formulation because 'l'article ainsi rédigé avait l'avantage de ne rien conclure, de ne rien désigner, de remettre seulement entre les mains de la société une arme pour la défendre, précisément sur le point où elle se trouverait blessée'.[13] Some députés supported this approach whole-heartedly. Georges Chabron de Solilhac, for example, held that 'c'est à l'opinion à réprimer les crimes et les écarts de l'opinion. Il faut pour de tels procès le jury'. Chabron's conception of public opinion was revealing:

> gardons-nous de confondre l'opinion publique avec l'opinion de la multitude [...] La véritable opinion publique [...] n'est pas le partage du grand nombre, elle se trouve dans les classes éclairées, chez les hommes qui ont des vertus et qui ont un grand intérêt à la conservation de l'ordre.[14]

12 *Moniteur Universel*, 19 April 1819, p. 3.

13 Quoted in J.-F. Carnot, *Examen des lois des 17, 26 mai, 9 juin 1819, et 31 mars 1820* (Paris: Nève, 1820), 26–7.

14 *Moniteur Universel*, 15 April 1819, p. 3.

If jurors were Chabron's men of order, jury trial might not protect dissidents such as Courier, but could indeed be prejudicial. Thus, after his conviction, Courier wrote to Mme Soehnée that the jury was 'la plus heureuse invention dont on se soit jamais avisé pour le despotisme'.[15]

The *Procès* itself falls into four parts: Courier's report of the opening of the trial (*OC*, 91–6; *Éc*, 285–9); his account of the prosecution case, which had been reported in full in the *Moniteur Universel* (*OC*, 96–105; *Éc*, 289–98); Berville's speech for the defence (*OC*, 105–25; *Éc*, 298–317); and the speech that Courier himself would have given, if he had not been dissuaded (*OC*, 126–34; *Éc*, 317–25). First the prosecution, led by the avocat général, Jacques-Nicolas de Broë. Naturally, he does not define 'outrage à la morale publique', but declares that the jury will be able to recognize the 'outrageous', as this is a 'vérité de sentiment'. He says of Courier's pages on the nobility: 'MM les jurés, vos cœurs nous ont répondu, et nous ne vous ferons pas l'injure d'une plus longue démonstration. Comme nous, vous déplorez de semblables écrits; comme nous, vous en sentez tous les dangers.'[16] However, he does extol the national worth of 'morale publique':

> Le plus précieux patrimoine d'un peuple est celui de la morale publique. C'est là qu'il trouve et les principes et les exemples qui le conduisent vers le bien et lui conservent ses forces et sa prospérité. [...] Le sentiment de l'honneur et l'amour de la liberté formèrent de tout tems le génie particulier, la noble passion des Français. Eh! bien, Messieurs, défendons-les ces généreux sentimens.[17]

The word 'exemples' in the second sentence confirms that de Broë wishes to defend the reputation of the Restoration's guiding elites.

His choice of targets within the *Discours* is similar. First, he states that the accused are not being prosecuted for criticizing the subscription, but 'pour avoir joint à la critique permise de cette souscription des allégations outrageantes pour la morale publique'.[18] The charge of 'outrage à la morale publique' concerns only four passages, but in practice, de Broë accuses

15 Letter 701 [214], 30 August 1821, CG III, 294.

16 *Moniteur Universel*, 29 August 1821, p. 4. When quoting de Broê verbatim, I follow the *Moniteur Universel*.

17 ibid.

18 ibid., p. 3.

the whole *Discours*. Thus, when he eventually reaches the first incriminated passage, he has already spent a quarter of his speech arguing that 'cet ouvrage a été dicté par un mauvais esprit et exprime des sentimens peu français' (ibid.). By talking of 'sentimens peu français' and implying lack of patriotism, de Broë exploits the 'national' perspective to insinuate that the entire text is an 'outrage à la morale publique'. His exordium reveals also that such a defence of 'morale publique' goes with fear of political instability. He recalls pre-Revolutionary propaganda, saying for example:

> on cherchait aussi à jetter sans cesse la défaveur sur l'emploi fait par le Roi de ses domaines, de ses apanages, de sa liste civile. Chaque matin paraissait un pamphlet destiné à prouver au peuple que son roi lui coûtait trop cher, et que la cupidité de la cour ne pouvait se comparer qu'à celle des prêtres. (Ibid.)

De Broë likens the *Discours* to these subversive texts, and condemns in Courier: 'un écrivain qui retombe dans des excès dont les effets sont connus et jugés [...] évidemment l'ennemi du repos de son pays'(ibid.). Though de Broë's focus is too broad and his expression excessive, the fear which he evokes is doubtless real. His attack conveys that the authorities thought Courier prominent enough to be dangerously subversive.

Finally reaching the 'outrageous' passages, the prosecutor asserts that they insult, respectively, clergy, monarchy, nobility, and legislators.[19]

19 As reported in the *Procès*, the passages cited were:

(a) 'Car la cour donne tout aux princes, comme les prêtres tout à Dieu; et ces domaines, ces apanages, ces listes civiles, ces budgets ne sont guère autrement pour le roi que le revenu des abbayes n'est pour Jésus-Christ. Achetez, donnez Chambord, c'est la cour qui le mangera; le prince n'en sera ni pis ni mieux' (*OC*, 100; *Éc*, 293. Cf. *Discours*, *OC*, 75; *Éc*, 264).

(b) 'Mais à Chambord', [le duc de Bordeaux] qu'apprend-il? Ce que peuvent enseigner et Chambord et la cour. Là, tout est plein de ses aïeux. Pour cela précisément je ne l'y trouve pas bien, et j'aimerais mieux qu'il vécût avec nous qu'avec ses ancêtres' (*OC*, 100; *Éc*, 293. Cf. *Discours*: *OC*, 78; *Éc*, 267).

(c) 'Sachez qu'il n'y a pas en France une seule famille noble, mais je dis noble de race et d'antique origine, qui ne doive sa fortune aux femmes; vous m'entendez. Les femmes ont fait les grandes maisons ; ce n'est pas, comme vous croyez bien, en cousant les chemises de leurs époux, ni en allaitant leurs enfants. [...] De la fortune des familles nobles il en paraît bien d'autres causes, telles que le pillage,

Courier mentions the clergy incidentally, amid a section on rapacious courtiers. However, the prosecutor highlights this aside, declares that it amounts to 'offenser calomnieusement et sans exception tous les ministres de nos saints autels', and that uttering such a libel is 'évidemment outrager la morale publique' (ibid.). On the monarchy, de Broë does not discuss passage (b), but emphasizes some subsequent pages. He alleges bias, in that Courier mentions only the immorality of François Ier and Louis XIV, not their achievements. Such criticism of some kings' morals can be an affront to 'morale publique', according to de Broë, for 'l'honneur de notre histoire et la gloire de nos rois forment la plus riche partie du patrimoine de la nation [...] si la gloire nationale est pour un peuple la première de toutes les propriétés, l'attaquer et l'outrager, c'est outrager, en même tems, la morale publique'.[20] Regarding passage (c), the prosecutor stresses that 'morale publique' includes the reputation of the aristocracy as a whole. He underlines heavily that Courier is vilifying a whole social class: for example, 'calomnier indignement une généralité d'individus [...] c'est, en

---

les concussions, l'assassinat, les proscriptions et surtout les confiscations. Mais qu'on y regarde, et on verra qu'aucun de ces moyens n'eût pu être mis en œuvre sans la faveur d'un grand, obtenue par quelque femme; car, pour piller, il faut avoir commandements, gouvernements, qui ne s'obtiennent que par les femmes; et ce n'était pas tout d'assassiner Jacques Cœur ou le maréchal d'Ancre, il fallait, pour avoir leurs biens, le bon plaisir, l'agrément du roi, c'est-à-dire des femmes qui gouvernaient alors le roi ou son ministre. Les dépouilles des huguenots, des frondeurs, des traitants, autres faveurs, bienfaits qui coulaient, se répandaient par les mêmes canaux aussi purs que la source. Bref, comme il n'est, ne fut, ni ne sera jamais, pour nous autres vilains, qu'un moyen de fortune, c'est le travail: pour la noblesse non plus, il n'y en a qu'un, et c'est ... c'est la prostitution' (*OC*, 101–2, *Éc*, 294–5. Cf. *Discours*, *OC*, 83; *Éc*, 271–2).

(d) 'O vous, législateurs nommés par les préfets, prévenez ce malheur (celui du morcellement des grandes propriétés); faites des lois, empêchez que tout le monde ne vive ! ôtez la terre au laboureur et le travail à l'artisan, par de bons privilèges, de bonnes corporations. Hâtez-vous, l'industrie, aux champs comme à la ville, envahit tout, chasse partout l'antique et noble barbarie. On vous le dit, on vous le crie: que tardez-vous encore? qui vous peut retenir? peuple, patrie, honneur? lorsque vous voyez là emplois, argent, cordons et le baron de Frimont' (*OC*, 103; *Éc*, 296. Cf. *Discours*, *OC*, 87; *Éc*, 275).

20 *Moniteur Universel*, 29 August 1821, p. 4.

un mot, outrager la morale publique. And similarly he exclaims: 'publier *qu'il n'y a pas en France une seule famille qui ne doive sa fortune à la prostitution*, c'est outrager de la manière la plus indigne la vérité, l'honneur des familles, la *morale publique*, en un mot'.[21] Passage (d) is Courier's ironic plea to the legislature to preserve estates that might be divided and sold to smallholders. De Broë, taking these lines to claim that the whole nation is servile, concludes: 'Accuser ainsi la France entière d'une lâche complaisance, d'une honteuse servilité, c'est encore outrager la morale publique.'[22] Courier certainly accuses legislators of venality and perhaps electors of supine deference to the executive, but de Broë's talk of 'la France entière' is excessive and revealing: because députés and voters were a few relatively wealthy men, he seems to equate 'la France entière' in effect with the rich. In practice, then, he considers each of the four passages in relation to an elite group with a role in society, and it is indeed their reputations which he is defending while alleging affronts to 'morale publique'.

Me Berville's speech underlined two radical flaws in this case. First, de Broë had not defined 'outrage à la morale publique' and, since he had not said what 'outrage' was, he could not *prove* that Courier had committed it. That omission also allowed Berville to define 'morale publique' as the rule of conscience innate in all mankind:

> cette morale absolue […] émanée de la Divinité, et supérieure à toutes les opinions humaines […] flétrit le mensonge, le larcin, le meurtre, l'impudicité: c'est celle-là seule qui prend le nom de morale *publique*, parce que, fondée sur l'assentiment de tous les hommes, elle a son témoignage, sa garantie, dans la conscience *publique*. (*OC*, 110–11; *Éc*, 303)

This definition is consistent with the 'universal' aspect of 'morale publique', as envisaged by the Garde des Sceaux. More importantly, it also implies that there are few conceivable offences against 'morale publique'. To transgress, an author would probably have to commend vice: thus, Berville inquires rhetorically, putting himself in Courier's place: 'ai-je fait l'apologie du vice?' (*OC*, 116; *Éc*, 308). Berville's second major objection

21 ibid.
22 ibid.

was to the idea that 'outrager une généralité, c'est outrager la morale publique' (as with the clergy or the nobility). Dismissing this position as absurd, he adds: 'je plains nos auteurs comiques. Désormais, il ne leur sera plus permis de dire, sous peine d'amende, [...] que les avocats sont bavards' (ibid.). Logically, his defence was strong and the prosecution case feeble, but he could not destroy it: he could not engage directly with de Broë's case because their ideas of 'morale publique' differed radically, and de Broë's idea was attuned to the jury's.

Courier's own imagined speech to the jury asserts, after Me Berville, that his criticisms of immorality and corruption are age-old and commonplace (*OC*, 121–2, 127; *Éc*, 313–14, 318). The prosecution, he declares, has two real purposes, neither related to 'morale publique'. First, a major aim is to avenge the nobility, for he had 'outragé ces classes distinguées de malfaisantes bêtes' (*OC*, 127; *Éc*, 318). Implicitly, his contention is supported by de Broë's speech, and the presiding judge's complaint: 'Vous avez outragé tout le corps de la noblesse' (*OC*, 95; *Éc*, 288). The second motive for the trial, Courier hints, is dynastic, and accordingly he urges the jurors to read some lines that were not explicitly incriminated: 'Feuilletez, Messieurs, lisez: *Un prince* ... Vous y voilà: *un jeune prince au collège* ... C'est cela même' (*OC*, 130; *Éc*, 321). Courier was well aware that his approving remarks about the Duc de Chartres at the Lycée Henri IV could suggest Orleanist sympathies, and that the suspicion of Orleanism could have helped inspire the prosecutors. Without openly accusing Courier of supporting the Duc d'Orléans, de Broë did allege disrespect for the Bourbons, deploring, for example, the bland terms in which Courier spoke of the Duc de Bordeaux: 'l'auteur trouve encore le moyen de ne parler du jeune prince, espoir de la patrie, que pour dire que son métier est de régner un jour'.[23] In reality, Orleanism was little threat to the Bourbons in 1821 and it remained marginal until after Charles X fell in 1830. But the Bourbons hated the Orléans, and this may have encouraged the prosecution, even if it was not the main motive.[24]

23 *Moniteur Universel*, 29 August 1821, p. 6.

24 Cobban, vol. 2, pp. 93–7; Teyssier, *Louis-Philippe*, IIe Partie; Benoît Yvert, 'Aux origines de l'Orléanisme. Les doctrinaires, *Le Globe* et les Bourbons', in *Guizot, les Doctrinaires et la presse* (Val Richer: Fondation Guizot, 1994), 11–33; Lautman, 197.

The first *Réponse aux anonymes* (1822) reiterates and develops Courier's idea that he had really been prosecuted for Orleanist sympathies. An imaginary correspondent tells him: 'on vous en veut, parce que vous êtes Orléaniste, ami particulier du duc d'Orléans. Vous l'avez loué dans quelques brochures, vous êtes du parti d'Orléans' (*OC*, 147; *Éc*, 376). Courier responds by praising the Duke for being progressive and patriotic: 'Il est de notre temps [...] Il a fait la guerre avec nous [...] et depuis, émigré malgré lui, jamais ne la fit contre nous' (*OC*, 152; *Éc*, 381). But the praise needs interpretation, since Courier says that he does not know the Duke personally and is echoing 'ce qui se dit' (*OC*, 153; *Éc*, 382). Avowed reliance on hearsay places a caveat alongside his approval, and suggests indeed that the text really serves to blame Louis XVIII, his brother, the future Charles X, and other *émigrés* for being reactionary or unpatriotic. Louis and Charles had, for example, been actively involved with the *émigré* forces that invaded France in 1792 to try to restore the monarchy. That critical aspect of Courier's remarks is the more prominent because he still denies political Orleanism: 'j'aime le duc d'Orléans; mais son ami, je ne le suis pas [...] Bien moins suis-je son partisan' (*OC*, 153–4; *Éc*, 382). Links between Courier and Louis-Philippe may have been closer than this passage suggests, but reliable evidence is lacking.[25] The denial matters also for the broader statement which follows: 'jamais je ne serai du parti de personne. Je ne suivrai pas un homme, ne cherchant pas fortune dans les révolutions, contre-révolutions qui se font au profit de quelques-uns' (*OC*, 154; *Éc*, 382). He assumes that men, some at least, adopt causes to make their own fortunes. Naming no names, he lets readers choose their own examples from the many available: for example, Fouché or Talleyrand, who usually contrived to be on the side of power, and thus served both Napoleon and Louis XVIII.[26] Courier's assertion of his own autonomy contrasts with such cases and recalls the praise that, in the second *Lettre particulière*, a neighbour bestowed on him for habitually defending oppressed parties: 'Aristocrate

25 *OC*, 951, n. 15; *Éc*, 383, n. 13. Courier went on lauding the Duke's qualities, while denying association with him, e.g. in the *Journal du Commerce*, 3 November 1823, *OC*, 205–6; *Éc*, 441.

26 Entries about alleged turncoats fill 400 pages in the satirical *Dictionnaire des girouettes* of 1815.

sous Robespierre, libéral en 1815' (*OC*, 64; *Éc*, 245). This is not quite the same as never belonging to any party but, as described in the *Lettre*, it does exclude permanent allegiance to any one faction. Even if Courier's denials of political partisanship may be idealized, they are at least consistent.

Another imaginary correspondent writes more broadly: 'vous n'aimez aucun prince, vous êtes républicain' (*OC*, 147; *Éc*, 376). Courier neither admits nor denies republicanism, but claims to be undecided about constitutions: 'J'ai lu de bons auteurs et réfléchi longtemps sur le meilleur gouvernement [...] plus je médite, et moins je sais à quoi m'en tenir' (*OC*, 147; *Éc*, 376–7). Courier's scepticism about forms of government is striking, since he had appreciated the *Charte Constitutionnelle*. However, as we noted earlier, he thought the mentality of police and judiciary more important than the institutional framework, and he already had radical misgivings about the effectiveness of the *Charte*. The first *Réponse* goes farther, condemning the document as fraudulent. A caustic page inspired by the fate of the *Discours* claims that the *Charte* exists to entrap potential opponents of the regime:

> La Charte vint, on me dit: Parlez, vous êtes libre, écrivez, imprimez; la liberté de la presse et toutes libertés vous sont garanties [...] Moi pauvre, qui ne connaissais pas le gouvernement provocateur [...] j'ouvre la bouche et je dis: Je voudrais, s'il vous plaisait, ne pas payer Chambord. Sur ce mot, on me prend, on me met en prison. (*OC*, 151; *Éc*, 380)

The expression 'gouvernement provocateur' is figurative here, as entrapment normally involves more positive steps to incite wrongdoing, but the allegation of deceit is far-reaching. Earlier regimes, Courier claims, had not used such devices: 'Bonaparte surtout [...] jamais ne nous leurra de la liberté de la presse ni d'aucune liberté' (*OC*, 150; *Éc*, 379).

Courier thought Restoration and Empire equally repressive, but here he notes that Napoleon was openly so. This ironic praise serves mainly to accuse the Restoration of hypocrisy. More broadly, after five regimes that were or became oppressive – Republic (Robespierre), Directory (Barras), Consulate (Bonaparte), Empire and Restoration – his scepticism over constitutional safeguards for freedom has implicitly the authority of experience.

The expressive devices used are particularly rich in *Aux âmes dévotes* and the *Procès*. We have seen the former reduce the *Discours* to eleven 'propositions scandaleuses, impies et révolutionnaires', satirically recalling a procedure favoured by intolerant theologians of the past who extracted suspect passages from texts that they wished to condemn (*Âmes*, *OC*, 89; *Éc*, 282). However, Paul-Louis was not facing theologians or defenders of morality but a host of parasites, united by hostility to himself:

> Le pauvre homme est en grande peine, ayant eu le malheur d'irriter contre lui tout ce qui s'appelle en France courtisans, serviteurs, flatteurs, adulateurs, complaisants, flagorneurs et autres gens vivant de bassesses et d'intrigues, lesquels sont au nombre, dit-on, de quatre ou cinq cent mille, tous enrégimentés sous diverses enseignes et déterminés à lui faire un mauvais parti. (*Âmes*, *OC*, 88; *Éc*, 281)

Here, the comedy lies partly in the numerical disproportion between this multitude and a lone individual. In detail, the text proceeds from terms that can be neutral ('courtisans, serviteurs') to others that are always pejorative ('adulateurs [...] flagorneurs') and bundles them all up dismissively as 'gens vivant de bassesses et d'intrigues'. This energetic list is also swept along by repetitions of sounds (-(t)eurs, fla-). The enumeration is comic in itself while more specifically conveying the onset of a motley horde, in which each seeks advancement by his own special form of 'bassesse' And this in turn suggests a further incongruity, that these varied competitors for favour are sufficiently united by hatred of the writer to form regiments, perhaps according to their specialities in 'bassesses' and 'intrigues'. Such comic lists may have rabelaisian echoes. The list above faintly recalls the île Farouche, where Pantagruel met a hostile army of sausages and puddings, 'Gigantales Andouilles [...] furieusement en bataille marchantes', which he estimated at 42,000, 'par la conjecture de soixante et dixhuict enseignes qu'il y comptoit'.[27] In this possibly rabelaisian context, the echo of Rabelais is amplified by alliteration: the sequence 'flatteurs, flagorneurs, flagornant par tout le royaume, etc. etc.' (*OC*, 91; *Éc*, 284) recalls the description of Frere Jean as a 'vray moyne si oncques en feut depuys que le monde moynant moyna de moynerie'.[28]

27 *Quart Livre* ch. 36, *Œuvres complètes*, 622–3.
28 *Gargantua* ch. 27 in *Œuvres complètes*, 78.

In their use of assonance and alliteration, Courier's lists are striking examples of verbal comedy, whether or not the reader thinks of Rabelais; however, if he does, then the comedy gains by association.[29]

In the *Procès*, Courier criticizes the prosecution case partly by caricaturing the prosecutor. He sometimes quotes de Broë's opening speech, but mainly summarizes it, on the grounds that it was too tedious and confused to reproduce, for fear of 'arrêter tout court mes lecteurs' (*OC*, 97; *Éc*, 290). As his summary highlights the internal contradictions and other deficiencies of de Broë's opening speech, it is a kind of parody, but one which follows the original quite closely. Two examples may suffice. First, de Broë invoked various passages not covered by the charge, and Courier shows the prosecutor himself admitting as much. Thus, he decries Courier's silences on the death of the Duc de Berry, or on the birth of the Duc de Bordeaux and then, 'après s'être étendu beaucoup sur tous ces points, maître de Broë déclare enfin qu'il ne s'agit pas de tout cela. Ce n'est pas là-dessus que porte l'accusation, dit-il' (*OC*, 99; *Éc*, 292). Similarly, de Broë quotes without comment the second allegedly immoral passage ('Mais à Chambord, qu'apprend-il?'), and condemns instead what follows in the *Discours*: 'Mais, dit-il, ensuite de ces phrases, il y en a d'autres horribles. Il ne les lira pas, parce qu'il n'en est point parlé dans l'acte d'accusation. Cependant, elles sont horribles' (*OC*, 100; *Éc*, 293). To ridicule this aspect of the speech, Courier simply recalled that de Broë indulged repeatedly and avowedly in irrelevant considerations ending, as above, in bathos. It is as if, here, Courier is simply letting the facts speak for themselves.

Courier also parodies de Broë's wordiness. How can he do so, without himself becoming verbose? His solution is exemplified in the paragraph below, which sums up de Broë's views on the fourth incriminated passage ('O vous, législateurs nommés par les préfets'):

> Accuser la nation d'une si lâche faiblesse, les préfets d'une telle audace, n'est-ce pas outrager à la fois à la morale publique et celle des préfets? Il faut donc venger la morale, qui est, dit maître de Broë, le patrimoine du peuple [...] et vengeons, punissons. Variations sur cet air: oui, punissons, vengeons. (*OC*, 103, *Éc*, 296)

29 Mireille Huchon, 'Courier lecteur de Rabelais', *Cahiers Paul-Louis Courier*, 2/4 (1980), 7–13.

Within limits, Courier does resort to mere repetition, using some form of the verb *venger* three times in four lines. More subtly, however, the mockery lies in the suggestion that de Broë was so wordy that he even produced variations on the pair 'vengeons, punissons'. Courier also emphasizes de Broë's wordiness by the implicit contrast with his own highly compressed style, as in the verbless sentence: 'Variations sur cet air'. The same telegraphic technique is applied, for example, to de Broë's reaction to the first incriminated passage: 'Tirade d'éloquence. [...] Tirades haut style sur la révolution. De morale, pas un mot, ni des phrases inculpées' (*OC*, 100; *Éc*, 293).

Finally, the caricature also recalls two fictitious orators in Rabelais. First, there is a parallel between de Broë and Dr Rondibilis in the *Tiers Livre*. Pantagruel's companion Panurge wants to marry but, fearing cuckoldry, asks various professionals for advice on this risk. Rondibilis takes a chapter and a half to advise that marriage and cuckoldry go naturally together, and that the cuckold must simply resign himself. Panurge dismisses his advice as useless verbiage: 'Vos parolles translatées de Barragouin en François voulent dire que je me marie hardiment, et que ne me soucie d'estre coqu. C'est bien rentré de treufles noires.'[30] Courier dismisses the prosecutor similarly, when he sets out to condense de Broë's speech, 'traduit de *baragouin* en français, comme dit Panurge' (*OC*, 98; *Éc*, 291). The second allusion is less explicit but seems inspired by *Gargantua* and the incompetent orator Janotus de Bragmardo, who pleads with Gargantua to return the bells of Notre Dame. Early in the account of de Broë's speech, small touches recall Janotus: 'maître Jean de Broë, prit la parole, ou, pour mieux dire, prit son papier, car il lisait' (*OC*, 96; *Éc*, 289). Renaming 'Jacques-Nicolas' 'Jean' may be a nod towards Janotus [= Janot = petit Jean]. Courier's pun 'prit la parole [...] prit son papier' highlights that the prosecutor relies on notes, as did Janotus. The parallel is mocking, for Janotus cannot decipher his own writing: unable to find a reference, he laments: 'si l'avoys je bien quotté en mon paperat'.[31] The term 'harangue' also recalls Janotus: in *Gargantua* his speech is 'la harangue de maistre Janotus'[32] and ironically 'sa belle harangue';[33] Courier normally employs the word 'discours'

30 *Tiers Livre*, ch. 34 in *Œuvres complètes*, 460.

31 *Gargantua*, ch. 19 in *Œuvres complètes*, 52.

32 ibid., ch. 19, p. 51.

33 ibid., ch. 18, p. 50.

but here he talks of 'la belle harangue de maître de Broë' (*OC*, 104; *Éc*, 296). The echoes of Janotus are faint but are amplified by the nearby allusion to Rondibilis. We may feel that de Broë is likened both to Rondibilis, who is long-winded and useless, and to Janotus, who is so incoherent and ineffectual that he can barely achieve verbosity. The parallels help give the caricature of de Broë a modest place amongst literary characters whose archetypal status goes beyond the needs of immediate satire. In Courier's mind, the figure of de Broë was central to the text: he calls the pamphlet his 'Jean de Broë', and underlines later that in it 'tout se réduit à dire que de Broë est un sot'.[34] The jury of course agreed with de Broë. If his performance was indeed so ridiculous, the divergence between it and the verdict highlights the injustice of the latter.

For Courier's place in the political history of the Restoration, the decision to prosecute him for the *Simple Discours* is significant. Whether the prosecution was really intended to protect the establishment's reputation, or to discourage praise of Louis-Philippe, or both, the proceedings unequivocally demonstrated the authorities' fear of Courier and his status in the political landscape of his day. In content, the *Simple Discours* highlights, more than any of Courier's other pamphlets, his defence of smallholding in association with anti-aristocratic sentiment and with moral considerations. The moral considerations, as we have noted, are not typically liberal, but rather reflect what Courier regarded as the real, practical constraints of the smallholders' existence. As for the aristocracy, the associated pamphlets are similarly hostile, perhaps *Aux âmes dévotes* more so. The accompanying texts also confirm that he was undecided about constitutions and hence not strictly anti-monarchist in principle; in practice, he distrusted the Bourbons and may have been warily sympathetic to Louis-Philippe. By their comic verve, *Aux âmes dévotes* and the *Procès* are outstanding. Their impact owes much to stylistic features, notably literary allusion and parody, and to a sense of absurdity, in that the *Discours*, which decries immorality is prosecuted for 'outrage à la morale publique'.

34 Letters to Mme Courier, 706 [215], 29–30 September 1821, *CG* III, 298; 724 [223], 8 November 1821, *CG* III, 319.

CHAPTER 4

Pamphlets, 1822–1823: Against the Pretensions of the Church

The post-Chambord pamphlets fall roughly into two groups. The *Pétition pour des villageois que l'on empêche de danser* and the second *Réponse aux anonymes*, centring on the Church, are examined in this chapter. The next chapter will consider the second group, largely on the Spanish question, with the *Pamphlet des pamphlets* (1824) as a general epilogue.

Before 1789, the Crown had been closely linked with the Church. The association was natural in a divine-right monarchy, where the Church sanctioned the King's status, most visibly at his coronation, and of course the crown also valued the clergy's role in upholding morality and social order.[1] Unsurprisingly, the restored monarchy tried to assist the Church, by legislative and other measures. Though Courier expresses no views on the Church's sacral role, he is highly critical of some measures in support of Catholicism and also takes a keen interest in the moral questions associated with the faith.

The Bourbons' intent to promote Catholicism was clear in the *Charte*, which guaranteed religious freedom, yet made Roman Catholicism the official religion:

> Art. 5 – Chacun professe sa religion avec une égale liberté et obtient pour son culte la même protection.
>
> Art. 6 – Cependant, la religion catholique, apostolique et romaine est la religion de l'État.[2]

1 Amongst influential contemporaries Chateaubriand, for one, thought Catholicism and the Church essential to the Crown (*De la monarchie selon la Charte*, 78–81, 90–4).

2 Rials, 50.

These Articles are contradictory: it is impossible to accord 'la même protection' to all religions, while conferring higher status on Catholicism. Catholic observance had in fact declined in the parishes: in Jussy-Champagne in Berry, for example, nearly all parishioners took Easter communion in 1789, but only half did so in 1814.[3] The Church sought to repair the situation, using its institutional preeminence with some success: for example, it launched numerous home missions supported by the secular authorities, and it secured oversight of schools. Courier ignores these developments, save to deride missions,[4] or attack Mgr Frayssinous as *grand maître de l'université*.[5] He mainly criticizes the *loi du 18 novembre 1814 concernant la célébration des Fêtes et Dimanches*, designed to protect Catholic observance.[6] The act limited or banned public entertainments on the days in question, particularly during the Mass, and required the civil power to enforce the measure: 'MM les préfets et sous-préfets, et sous leurs ordres les commissaires de police, les officiers de paix, sont chargés de tenir la main à son exécution' (Art. 13).[7] When, on the strength of this act, the new parish priest in Azay-sur-Cher, Pierre-Alexandre Bruneau, obtained an *arrêté préfectoral* against dancing on Sundays, Courier's reaction was the *Pétition pour des villageois que l'on empêche de danser*.[8]

This text was not a petition to the legislature but a pamphlet against joint interventions in everyday life by Church and State. According to Courier,

> Le curé d'Azai [...] attaqua la danse, et semble avoir promis à Dieu de l'abolir dans sa paroisse, usant pour cela de plusieurs moyens, dont le principal et le seul efficace, jusqu'à présent, est l'autorité du préfet. Par le préfet, il réussit à nous empêcher de danser, et bientôt nous fera défendre de chanter et de rire. (*OC*, 140; *Éc*, 348)

3 Tulard, *Les Français sous Napoléon*, 109.
4 *LCens VI*, *OC*, 22; *Éc*, 195; *Lpart* (2), *OC*, 69; *Éc*, 250; *Gazette*, *OC*, 179–80; *Éc*, 416.
5 *Livret*, *OC*, 166–7; *Éc*, 402.
6 On religious revival under the Restoration, see Waresquiel, 'La Charte, le sacre et le droit divin', in *Penser la Restauration*, 215–40; Bertier, 300–24; and, for a more sceptical assessment, Price, 117–19.
7 Text in Lautman, 267–8.
8 Lautman, 212; *Éc*, 339.

The case clearly involves Courier's idea about personal freedom, that the authorities should not intervene in the sphere of private life, whence such remarks as: 'c'est chez soi qu'on a droit de danser; et où le public sera-t-il chez lui, sinon sur la place publique?' (*OC*, 139; *Éc*, 347). Referring to a village square, the argument is specious, since a square is not private like a family's home. But the device of treating the public as if it were a family confirms Courier's thinking: such pastimes, while open to all, belong rather to private life and should remain beyond the authorities' reach. The *Pétition aux deux Chambres* had already deplored oppressive policing. This text suggests that executive support of the Church further expands the police state: 'Les gendarmes se sont multipliés [...] le gouvernement est partout aujourd'hui, et cette *ubiquité* s'étend jusqu'à nos danses, où il ne se fait pas un pas dont le préfet ne veuille être informé' (*OC*, 135; *Éc*, 344). As in the *Pétition aux deux Chambres*, Courier appeals to the reader's sense of disproportion – here, between 'danse et [...] amusements' (*OC*, 134; *Éc*, 343) and the repressive machine used against them.

The *loi du 18 novembre 1814* also stipulated that 'les travaux seront interrompus les dimanches et les jours de fêtes' (Art. 1), a significant restriction of freedom to work. The role of land and work in improving life for the post-Revolutionary peasant had been emphasized in the *Simple Discours* as in *Lettres V-VI au 'Censeur'*, and this *Pétition* returns to the theme, quoting La Bruyère's description of the peasantry:

> certains animaux farouches [...] répandus dans la campagne, noirs, livides, nus, et tout brûlés du soleil, attachés à la terre qu'ils fouillent et remuent avec une opiniâtreté invincible [...] se retirent la nuit dans des tanières, où ils vivent de pain noir, d'eau et de racines. (*OC*, 138; *Éc*, 346)[9]

Courier notes that, if La Bruyère searched now for the peasants of his day, 'ces animaux dont il a fait la description, il ne les trouverait nulle part' (*OC*, 139; *Éc*, 347). The mutation of brutishness into humanity is a striking image of social progress between the seventeenth and nineteenth centuries.

9 Jean de La Bruyère, *Les Caractères*, ed. Robert Pignarre (Paris: Garnier-Flammarion, 1965), ch. 12; 'De l'Homme', 128, p. 292.

For Courier, then, the *loi* threatens both the peasants' liberty and their material condition. He develops his criticism by recalling that holy days once protected serfs: 'Quand l'Église a fait ce commandement de s'abstenir à certains jours de toute œuvre servile, il y avait des serfs alors liés à la glèbe [...] le précepte fut sage et la loi salutaire dans ces temps d'oppression' (*OC*, 137; *Éc*, 345–6). But now the demand to observe feasts and Sundays is regressive and inhumane, as it ignores the transformation wrought by the Revolution and the peasant owners' changed burdens in this life. Courier notes the contention that religious observance concerns an overriding interest, the salvation of the soul: 'Nos dévots [...] voudraient que, ce jour-là, on ne fît rien du tout que prier et dire ses heures. C'est la meilleure chose et la seule nécessaire, l'affaire du salut' (*OC*, 137; *Éc*, 345). Without explicitly rejecting this view, he puts the counter-argument of necessity. The statute itself allows exceptions for 'travaux de la moisson et des récoltes que l'état de la saison ou la crainte des intempéries rendraient urgents' (Art. 9). Though the legislator probably envisaged only rare cases when bad weather threatened the harvest, the law implicitly bolstered Courier's position, by providing that necessity could in principle justify departures from the rule. For Courier, however, the necessity is permanent: the peasants must toil constantly to satisfy the establishment's own fiscal greed:

> le percepteur est là; il faut payer et travailler pour ceux qui ne travaillent point [...] enfants, vieillards, mendiants, moines, laquais, courtisans; que de gens à entretenir [...] ceux qui haïssent tant le travail du dimanche veulent des traitements, envoient des garnisaires, augmentent le budget. (Ibid.)

Courier objects then to the authorities' inconsistency, while invoking his own schematic distinction between the active and the idle. But he also stresses the conflict between the statute and the changed values of peasants whom he thinks largely dechristianized. Again he contrasts past and present:

> Esclave auparavant, il [le peuple] prenait du loisir, pouvait [...] penser au ciel, où était son espoir, sa consolation. Maintenant il pense à la terre qui est à lui, et le fait vivre. Dans le présent ni dans l'avenir, le paysan n'envisage plus qu'un champ, une maison qu'il a ou veut avoir, pour laquelle il travaille. (*OC*, 142; *Éc*, 350)

Where once peasants had focused on a spiritual afterlife, they have become materialistic and uninterested in religion, and the act feels all the more oppressive because it imposes restrictions to protect a faith now alien to the peasant outlook.

Courier's own religious views are less reductive, as they appear in his *Lettre à MM. de l'Académie* (1819). In the *Lettre*, a pamphlet which he wrote after failing to gain election to the Académie des Inscriptions et Belles-Lettres, he suggests that the Académie had rejected him partly because he was not an overtly practising Catholic. In this connection, he outlines his personal principles, beginning with his epistemology:

> Mes principes sont *qu'entre deux points la ligne droite est la plus courte; que le tout est plus grand que sa partie; que deux quantités, égales chacune à une troisième, sont égales entre elles.* Je tiens aussi *que deux et deux font quatre*; mais je n'en suis pas bien sûr. Voilà mes principes, messieurs, dans lesquels j'ai été élevé, grâce à Dieu, et dans lesquels je veux vivre et mourir. (*OC*, 283; *Éc*, 161)

This pronouncement is sceptical: Courier limits what can be known with certainty to axiomatic propositions; and, even here, he claims that there may be room for doubt over some propositions, such as the sum of two plus two. As the sum of two and two is proverbially obvious, Courier is underlining his own scepticism very heavily. The final formula about 'principes [...] dans lesquels je veux vivre et mourir' would usually be applied to a religious credo. While such displacement may be mildly parodic, the formula also indicates that these principles really are fundamental to his outlook. He goes on from epistemology to his own religion: 'La foi du centenier, la foi du charbonnier sont passées en proverbe. Je suis soldat et bûcheron, c'est comme charbonnier' (ibid.). The 'centenier' is the centurion who pleaded with Jesus to save his dying servant: 'Je ne mérite pas que tu entres sous mon toit; mais dis seulement un mot et mon serviteur sera guéri' (Matthew 8. 8). The centurion, then, exemplifies simple faith and humility. The *foi du charbonnier* is also, as Courier says, proverbially unsophisticated. Apt though these parallels are to Courier's employments, do they tell us anything about his religion? He never quite says that he shares the centurion's faith. At first glance, Courier's sceptical principles may indeed seem to preclude religious faith, but epistemological scepticism and faith can be allied, in theory at least, as in the doctrine of fideism. Put simply, the fideist argument is that reason can tell men little or nothing about the natural world, and still less about the supernatural; reason cannot tell men, for example, whether God exists or not. Consequently, it is not reasonable to say that God exists, and not reasonable to say that He does not exist. In these circumstances, men accept or reject religious beliefs by an act of will rather than by reason. In Courier's case, because his other writings show so little personal interest in faith, it is very difficult to see him as a believer, even on a fideist basis. While agreeing that there is no rational knowledge of the supernatural, he might logically have opted neither to affirm nor to deny the existence of the supernatural and opted for an agnostic position.[10]

Because his contemporaries so readily associated religion and morality, Courier also enunciates his own moral code, which contains one rule: 'Ne point faire à autrui ce que je ne voudrais pas qui me fût fait' (*OC*, 284; *Éc*, 161). This is the negative version of the so-called 'Golden Rule'. The positive formulation of the rule appears in Christian teaching: 'Tout ce que vous désirez que les autres fassent pour vous, faites-le vous-mêmes pour eux' (Matthew 7. 12). However, whether in its negative or positive form, the Rule occurs in the non-religious moral teachings of various writers such as Isocrates, whose works Courier certainly knew.[11] It is independent of religious faith, and such is no doubt the main point for Courier. Though this is not the place to examine the Golden Rule in detail, we may add that it has its limitations, because its application depends on individuals' personal, subjective assessments of what is desirable or tolerable. For example, I may wish others to refrain from lying to me and, on Courier's version of the Golden Rule, I must refrain from lying to others. But it is conceivable that someone else, while also subscribing to Courier's Rule, might think it tolerable that others lie to him, and hence feel that Courier's Rule does not prevent his telling his own lies. The Rule is more secure in extreme cases, such as homicide: men generally would not wish to be murdered, and

10 But Gaschet thought him a sincere believer, albeit 'plus que tiède pour la pratique du culte' (p. 170).

11 Isocrates *Nicocles* (Cambridge, MA: Harvard U. P. (Loeb Classical Library), 1928). Isocrates, vol. I Section 61.

Courier's Rule would then forbid them to murder others. The importance of the Rule in Courier's thinking will become particularly clear when he sets out to prove that men can be pious and exceedingly evil at the same time (*Rép* (2), *OC*, 159–60; *Éc*, 387–9).

Reverting to the peasants, we find Courier sharing their religious indifference: 'nous ne sommes pas de ces tièdes que Dieu vomit, [...] nous sommes froids' (*OC*, 143; *Éc*, 350). Such apathy is consistent with the agnosticism implied by the *Lettre à MM. de L'Académie* but, unlike the peasants no doubt, he sees that obsession with material goods is perilous: the *Gazette du Village* (1823) reports that some peasants work themselves to death, like Moreau and his wife (*OC*, 178; *Éc*, 415), while others kill themselves in despair: 'On aime mieux maintenant être mort que ruiné. Nos aïeux ne se tuaient point. Naissant pour la misère, ils la savaient souffrir' (*OC*, 182; *Éc*, 418). Though welcoming the peasants' material and social progress, he recognizes that narrow materialism did not always bring them happiness or fulfilment.[12] Liberal thinkers, though generally less Catholic than royalists, did not necessarily dismiss religious belief, and in taking it seriously Courier did not diverge from them. His unease over peasant materialism anticipates, for example, Constant's view that even the man who is materially successful needs religion: 'il a tout connu, tout calculé, et il éprouve de la lassitude à ne s'être occupé que d'intérêts et de calculs. Une voix crie au fond de lui-même [...] que ce qu'il a pris pour un but n'était qu'une série de moyens'.[13]

Regarding the Church's efforts to revive Catholicism, Courier judged the clergy's aggressive methods to be futile. The priests must, he writes, follow such biblical texts as '*Je suis doux et humble de cœur*. On ramènerait ainsi des brebis égarées que trop de rigueur effarouche' (*Villageois*, *OC*, 144; *Éc*, 352). His model is the elderly parish priest in Véretz, 'ami de la jeunesse, trop raisonnable pour vouloir la réformer sur le patron des âges passés'

12 But Auerbach claims that this godless desert with material gain as men's only motivation was Courier's political ideal: 'Alle Kräfte der menschlichen Seele gründet er auf den Egoismus des bürgerlichen Eigentümers [...] dieses von aller Welt und von Gott abgesonderte [...] Menschenwesen [...] ist allen Ernstes Couriers politisches Ideal' (p. 530).

13 *De la religion* in Benjamin Constant, *Œuvres*, 1379.

(*OC*, 140; *Éc*, 348). Such wisdom is rare, especially in new priests from the Tours seminary who 'veulent extirper d'abord tout plaisir' (*OC*, 141; *Éc*, 349). When confessing young women, their object is puritanical and their method coercive: they grant absolution only to women who promise to give up dancing. The result is a fiasco, with the numbers at Mass falling by over three quarters (*OC*, 142; *Éc*, 350). Such coercion reflects individual priests' misguided zeal and also the Church's authoritarian tradition:

> Ce n'est pas [...] d'aujourd'hui, que les ministres de l'Église ont eu la pensée de s'aider du bras séculier dans la conversion des pécheurs, où les apôtres n'employaient que l'exemple et la parole, selon le précepte du maître. Car Jésus avait dit: Allez et instruisez. Mais il n'avait pas dit: Allez avec des gendarmes, instruisez de par le préfet. (*OC*, 140; *Éc*, 348).

The Church's resort to duress, sometimes in alliance with the secular powers, is ineffectual and un-Christian. By highlighting this incoherence, the texts convey disdain for the Church as an institution. The *Pétition* is Courier's main attack on clerical authoritarianism.

The *Pétition* brought him a second prosecution, this time for *outrage à la religion de l'État, outrage à la morale publique et religieuse, provocation à la désobéissance à la loi du 18 novembre 1814*, and *provocation à la haine et au mépris du gouvernement du Roi*. He was acquitted because the court found that the relevant passages, though blameworthy, did not contravene the legislation.[14] Three points deserve particular mention. First, the fact that Courier was prosecuted again and the case again reported in the *Moniteur* confirms his standing as a controversialist. He begins the *Pétition* by recalling his recent release from prison (*Éc*, 343), which leads the prosecutor Me Billot to inveigh against

> un écrivain [...] qui déjà condamné pour semblable délit, pousse le cynisme de la sédition et de l'outrage au point de rappeler lui-même en tête de son nouveau libelle, comme un moyen de recommandation auprès de ses lecteurs, le châtiment que la justice lui a une première fois infligé.

14 *Moniteur universel*, 27 novembre 1822, p. 4. See *Éc* 341–2.

In emotive terms which confirm how much the authorities feared Courier and wished to silence him, Billot demands severe punishment for

> celui qui, de sang froid et en se jouant, sappe [sic] toutes les bases de la société. Lorsque regardant autour de vous, vous apercevez le trône encore fumant de la foudre révolutionnaire, n'oubliez pas qu'avant d'éclater, c'est dans des écrits impies et séditieux qu'elle s'était formée.

The second point concerns Courier's alleged target. Fear that the *Pétition* and its like may undermine authority and encourage another revolution echoes the anxiety expressed by de Broë during the first trial. But here an additional dimension is that Billot wholly assimilates the standing of the Church with that of the Crown: to attack the former is to attack the latter. Thirdly, under new legislation, there was no longer a jury at this type of trial. As the magistrates acquitted Courier, he did not suffer from the absence of jurors. The point is incidental here, but its general importance will appear in connection with the *Pamphlet des pamphlets*.

As for the clergy's moral role, the text concedes that Catholic priests of the new generation are morally exemplary (*OC*, 144; *Éc*, 351). In earlier pamphlets, Courier had highlighted clerical decadence, usually in *émigré* priests who had returned at the Restoration. The improbably named Jean Chouart is typical[15]: a good priest before emigrating, he came back a 'hussard en soutane, dont le hardi regard fait rougir nos jeunes filles, et dont la langue sème le trouble et la discorde [...] Tels sont nos prêtres de retour de l'émigration (*LCens* VI, *OC*, 26; *Éc*, 198). The next letter suggests that some returning priests are obsessed with regaining their pre-Revolutionary status and income. Thus the grand vicaire de S ..., after years of womanizing and theft abroad, now thinks only of recovering his position. When asked what he thought about some major theological issues, he is dismissive: 'Je pense, répondit-il en colère, à ravoir mon prieuré' (*LCens* VII, *OC*, 28–9; *Éc*, 201).

15 Jean Chouart is the name of greedy priest in *Le Curé et le mort* (*Fables*, 7, x). It also echoes Panurge's uncouth overtures to a Parisian lady: 'Tenez (monstrant sa longue braguette) voicy maistre Jan Chouart qui cherche logis' (Rabelais, *Pantagruel*, in *Œuvres complètes*, 295).

The second *Réponse aux anonymes* suggests that, while the new priests behave better than their precursors, it is despite two major burdens imposed by Catholicism: confession and clerical celibacy. These practices had been contested when the sixteenth-century Reformers tried to restore Christianity to what they took to be the teachings of the Bible and the customs of the first-century Church. The Reformers rejected later changes of doctrine or practice, including confession and celibacy, as inventions of men, and especially of popes. Thus Calvin accuses the papacy of spreading 'nouvelles doctrines pour destourner le povre peuple de la pure simplicité de la parolle de Dieu'.[16] In removing 'nouvelles doctrines', Reformed churches generally allowed clerical marriage, and restricted or abolished individual confession. Courier's view is worth quoting at length:

> quelles sources d'impuretés, de désordres, de corruption, que ces deux inventions du pape, le célibat des prêtres et la confession nommée auriculaire! que de mal elles font! que de bien elles empêchent! Il le faut voir et admirer, là où la famille du prêtre est le modèle de toutes les autres [...] les femmes n'ont point l'impudence de dire à un homme leurs péchés; le clergé n'est point hors du temple, hors de l'État, hors de la loi; tous abus établis chez nous dans les temps de la plus stupide barbarie, de la plus crédule ignorance, difficiles à maintenir aujourd'hui que le monde raisonne. (*Rép* (2), *OC*, 164; *Éc*, 393)

The expression 'inventions du pape' sounds Protestant, as does Courier's praise of married clergymen, and he clearly appreciates these aspects of Protestantism. However, he remains a rationalist, whence the contrast between two eras: 'les temps de la plus stupide barbarie, de la plus crédule ignorance,' and the present when 'tout le monde raisonne'. This contraposition echoes the liberal belief in mankind's intellectual progress without, however, the faith in progress expressed most eloquently by Mme de Staël and, to some extent, by Constant. Here again, as in *Lettre IX au 'Censeur'* the text limits reason to a strictly critical role.

Where the *Pétition* criticizes the coercive use of confession, the second *Réponse* dwells on the distress of young priests who, when confessing young women, suffer conflicts between 'la défense de posséder ce que nature les

16 Jean Calvin, *Institution de la religion chrestienne*, ed. Jacques Pannier, 4 vols (Paris: Les Belles-Lettres, 1961), vol. 4, p. 182.

force d'aimer, et l'obligation de converser intimement, confidemment, avec ces objets de leur amour' (*OC*, 162; *Éc*, 391). The question of confession is subordinated here to that of priestly celibacy. To illustrate the pain involved in celibacy, Courier recalls two Italians, Canon Fortini and an unnamed priest in Rocca di Papa, who had befriended him and eventually admitted their woe. Fortini concludes: 'J'ai souffert, Dieu le sait, et m'en tiendra compte, j'espère; mais je ne recommencerais pas.' To this sober verdict, Courier adds: 'Voilà ce qu'il me dit, et je notai ce discours si bien dans ma mémoire, que je me rappelle ses propres mots' (*OC*, 162; *Éc*, 391–2). With the other priest, Courier jests:

> Cher abbé, demain je me confesse, si tu veux te marier et vivre heureux. Tu ne peux l'être qu'avec une seule femme, et je sais celle qu'il te faut. Tu la vois chaque jour, tu l'aimes, tu péris. Il me mit la main sur la bouche, et je vis que ses yeux se remplissaient de pleurs. (*OC*, 162–3; *Éc*, 392)

Courier begins in a light tone but ends with a moment of pathos rare in his writing. These passages suggest real pity for the plight of certain Catholic priests.

As regards enforced celibacy Courier also considers the risk that it will produce serious depravity, as in the case of Antoine Mingrat. Mingrat really existed and, having been born in 1794, he belonged to the new generation of priests whose personal morality Courier had recently acknowledged. But Mingrat was an exception. He was puritanical in public, condemned dancing on Sundays and feast days, and demanded decency in women's dress (*Rép.* (2), *OC*, 155–6; *Éc*, 385–6). But some whispered that he had fathered several children, and perhaps murdered a female parishioner.[17] Amid such rumours, his superiors transferred him from the parish of Saint-Aupre to Saint-Quentin (Isère), where he continued as before. In public, he 'fit la guerre plus que jamais à la danse et aux manches de chemise'; in private, having become the confessor of a beautiful young woman, he killed her, cut up her body, and dumped it in the Isère (*OC*, 158; *Éc*, 388). For Courier, Mingrat exemplifies both the suffering and the evil which enforced celibacy

17 Jean-Pierre Lautman, 'L'Affaire Mingrat: origines et répercussions d'une offensive contre l'Église', *Cahiers Paul-Louis Courier*, 4/6 (2010), 79–116 (p. 98).

may cause: 'Je trouve dans son état de prêtre de quoi, non l'excuser, mais le plaindre. Il n'eût pas tué assurément sa seconde maîtresse, s'il eût pu épouser la première devenue grosse, et qu'il a tuée aussi, selon toute apparence' (*OC*, 155; *Éc*, 385).

The episode also raises basic questions about the nature of piety. Being puritanical in public, lecherous in private, Mingrat seems merely hypocritical. But Courier disagrees, and supports his judgment with a startling example:

> Vous l'appelez hypocrite; moi, je le crois dévot, sincère et de bonne foi. La dévotion s'allie à tout. Lorsqu'on fait en Italie assassiner son ennemi, cela coûte vingt ou dix ducats, selon qu'on veut le damner ou qu'on ne le veut pas. Pour ne le point damner, on lui dit avant de le tuer: Recommande ton âme à Dieu; pardonne-moi et fais un acte de contrition. Il dit son *in manus*, pardonne, et on l'égorge; il va en paradis. Mais voulant le damner, on s'y prend autrement. Il faut tâcher de le trouver en péché mortel; et pour le plus sûr, on lui dit, le poignard levé: Renie Dieu, ou je te tue. Il renie, on le tue, et il va en enfer. (*OC*, 159–60; *Éc*, 389)

It is manifestly un-Christian to murder one's enemies or try to contrive their damnation. But equally un-Christian is the belief that salvation can be lost mechanically, as when the victim's mere words, spoken under duress, are taken to damn him irrevocably and to exclude even divine mercy. Yet, according to Courier, such murderous acts and such bizarre beliefs can coexist with sincere piety, if piety is defined as strict fidelity to external practices prescribed for Roman Catholics: 'Ces choses se font tous le jours, là où personne ne voudrait, pour rien au monde, avoir goûté d'un potage gras le vendredi. Voilà la dévotion vraie, naïve, non feinte, non suspecte d'hypocrisie' (*OC*, 160; *Éc*, 389).[18]

Though the text describes a deviant form of piety, this assault on 'dévotion' is significant because, once again, its ultimate target is the idea that Christianity is essential to morality. After letting this version of Italian piety condemn itself, Courier adds cuttingly: 'La morale, dit-on, est fondée

18 Courier presumably thought that Italian and Savoyard peasants – unlike his own neighbours – were amongst the 'pious'. They would have been too poor to hire assassins, but Courier's letters show Italian peasants convinced that killing Frenchmen was a 'bonne œuvre' (107 [29], 23 April 1805, *CG* I, 187).

là-dessus' (ibid.). If 'la dévotion s'allie à tout', as Courier contends, it is indeed unsafe to base any morality on such foundations. Courier's point here is to attack the alleged dependence of morality on Christianity, not to put forward alternatives, and he does not refer to his own guiding principle: 'Ne point faire à autrui ce que je ne voudrais pas qui me fût fait' (*Acad*, *OC*, 284; *Éc*, 161). However, we are free to ask how that rule would have applied in the Italian example. As we have noted, the rule is subjective, for it depends on each individual's idea of what he would not want done to himself. However, we may assume that no one would wish or consent to be murdered, or to be murdered in a way intended to precipitate him into eternal damnation. If guided by Courier's principle, then, no one would inflict such treatment on others. In short, 'Ne point faire à autrui ...' would have excluded the atrocious cruelty which a form of piety permits. Such cases, albeit extreme, would certainly argue against Christian piety as the necessary basis for moral behaviour. Earlier, Courier had contended that piety was not necessary for morality; here, his text tends to show that piety is not only unnecessary but may also be pernicious if it excuses major failings, as appears further in Mingrat's case.

After Mingrat's second crime, the mayor of Saint-Quentin investigated and reported his action, but his ecclesiastical superiors tried to protect him. At least one sermon insinuated that the husband was the murderer, and also that Mingrat had learnt the truth from the husband, but could not use it to defend himself because he had received the information in confession. Mingrat is thus transmuted into 'un martyr du secret de la confession'. His 'martyrdom' is implausible, since this account could not have emerged unless he had in fact breached the secret of confession; however, pious opinion supported the tale. Eventually, despite such backing and the reluctance of the civil authorities to arrest a priest, Mingrat had to flee from French jurisdiction to the Kingdom of Piedmont. In his absence he was convicted of murder and sentenced to death by the Cour d'assises in Grenoble (*OC*, 159; *Éc*, 388–9). Meanwhile, the Piedmontese authorities incarcerated him in the fortress of Fenestrelle, where he received pious visitors:

> il passe pour un saint et fait des miracles. On vient à lui de la vallée, de la montagne, en pèlerinage; on accourt, les femmes surtout, le voir, lui demander sa bénédiction. Cette main les bénit; il leur tend cette main qu'elles baisent, femmes et filles, sans

> penser, sans frémir, sachant ce qu'il a fait, car d'un lieu si voisin, personne ne l'ignore. Mais on lui pardonne beaucoup, parce qu'il a beaucoup aimé; ou peut-être il se repent, et dès lors il vaut mieux que quatre-vingt-dix-neuf justes. Qu'il en confesse encore quelqu'une jeune, jolie, et qu'elle lui résiste, il en fera comme des autres, sans perdre pour cela le paradis. (*OC*, 159; *Éc*, 389)

The last sentence implies that Mingrat might be released and allowed to resume his ministry. This seems not to have happened, but such an outcome was conceivable, given the Church's earlier treatment of the affair. That said, three major points emerge from these lines. First, there is the credulity of Mingrat's devotees, who accept that he is saintly, despite what they know of his deeds. In context, the implication is presumably that blinding piety makes them gullible. The second point concerns the sentence beginning 'Mais on lui pardonne ...', which suggests that, in credulous minds, Mingrat's position is further bolstered by an apparent analogy with the biblical stories of Mary Magdalen, whose sins were forgiven because she had 'beaucoup aimé' (Luke 7. 36–47), and of the lost sheep (Matthew 18. 19). Mary Magdalen was a prostitute, but a repentant one; 'beaucoup aimé' does not concern her former trade but her love for Jesus. Mingrat's love, on the other hand, consisted of seducing parishioners, and his repentance, if any, was surely superficial, as his behaviour seems never to have changed.[19] Thus, the gullibility of the believers is further underscored by their acceptance of a misplaced allusion to Mary Magdalen. The third point arises with the parable of the one sheep that was lost and the ninety-nine that never strayed. The parable seems to be about Jesus's love for the repentant sinner whom he saves. In principle this is certainly applicable to the sinner Mingrat, who could still repent and be saved from damnation. The problem is rather the idea that, if he repented, he would have greater worth than ninety-nine just men. The subject pronoun 'on' in these sentences certainly designates the pious laity; but no doubt it refers also to clerics, following the hierarchy's policy of exalting Mingrat. However, by human standards, whether Mingrat repented or not, he is

19 Christian definitions of repentance must be left to specialists. However, true repentance seems to involve a total change of conduct and of spirit (Calvin, *Institution chrestienne*, vol. 2, pp. 175–6).

a depraved man who wrought havoc amongst parishioners entrusted to him, and any belief in his superior worth is preposterous: as a precaution he should be isolated from the faithful and, as a matter of justice, guillotined. The third point, then, is that the position of the Church and the values of men may clash irrevocably. For Courier, as a rationalist and perhaps an agnostic, human values must be supreme.

Two persuasive methods are particularly notable in these pamphlets. The first is recourse to the authority of the Bible. Sometimes, as we have just seen, Courier explicitly quotes Scripture against the Church's attempts at compulsion: '*Je suis doux* … '(Matthew 11. 29; *Villageois*, *OC*, 144; *Éc*, 352) and 'Allez et instruisez …' (Matthew 28. 19; *OC*, 140; *Éc*, 348). These quotations are clearly pertinent to the issues, as is no doubt a reference to St Paul, which Courier uses against the Church's outmoded attachment to saints' days, 'la lettre tue …' (II Corinthians 3. 6; *OC*, 137; *Éc*, 345). Other allusions to Scripture, though less obviously relevant, may also have some bearing on the issues. When, in a rather obscure passage, St Paul counsels discernment (I Corinthians 12. 10), he may be advising the faithful to discern between the various spirits which inspire religious zeal; but Courier takes it as advice to the zealots themselves that they must exercise their zeal with discretion (*OC*, 142; *Éc*, 350). A reference to David dancing for joy before the Ark of God (II Samuel 6. 14–16) is barely relevant, but at least suggests that dance is not unholy *per se* (*OC*, 144–5; *Éc*, 352).

Not only does Courier make positive use of Scripture for his own case, but he also contends that other references are misused by the Church, as we have just seen in the cases of Mary Magdalen and the prodigal son. Obviously, for many centuries, religious controversialists have advanced arguments based on Scripture. But what Courier is doing is something more subversive: not only is he advancing a religious argument but he is also seeking to confound the Church as an institution by suggesting that it is at odds with the very authority which supposedly justifies its sway in the world. This radical inconsistency may be due partly to clerical duplicity, but perhaps also to clerical ignorance. Thus, Courier ironically warns the *académiciens* against the demands of the learned that teachers should understand what they teach: 'sait-on où cela s'arrêterait ? Bientôt ceux qui prêchent l'Évangile seraient obligés de l'entendre' (*Acad.*, *OC*, 279; *Éc*, 157).

It is somewhat unusual for Courier to exploit Scripture, as in the *Pétition pour des villageois* and the second *Réponse aux anonymes*. However, for him to use a written authority closely associated with his adversaries is in itself characteristic enough. Here, as with the Charte, this resource helps him to buttress his own positions or at least to highlight his opponents' inconsistencies.

The second notable feature is the persuasive use of narrative, the appeal to the reader's imagination as much as to his reason. In making the case against clerical celibacy, the text maintains that extreme tension arises between human nature and the vow of chastity. To promote this view, Courier imagines a debate with one of his anonymous correspondents, who is taken to condemn Mingrat, on the basis that it would have been possible for him to observe his vows and behave correctly. To persuade the correspondent that chastity and human nature normally conflict – and that Mingrat's is simply an extreme case – Courier invites him to imagine a priest confessing a woman whom he loves:

> lorsqu'il l'entend [...] approcher de ce confessional, qu'il reconnaît ses pas et qu'il peut dire: C'est elle, que se passe-t-il dans l'âme du pauvre confesseur? [...] il frémit, il désire, et déjà malgré lui, sans le savoir peut-être, il espère. Elle arrive, se met à ses genoux, à genoux devant lui dont le cœur saute et palpite. Vous êtes jeune, Monsieur, ou vous l'avez été; que vous semble entre nous d'une telle situation? Seuls, la plupart du temps, et n'ayant pour témoins que ces murs, que ces voûtes, ils causent; de quoi? hélas! de tout ce qui n'est pas innocent. Ils parlent, ou plutôt murmurent à voix basse, et leurs bouches s'approchent, leur souffle se confond. Cela dure une heure ou plus, et se renouvelle souvent. (*Rép* (2), *OC*, 161; *Éc*, 390–1)

A distinctive aspect of the narrative is that initially, it identifies more or less directly with the impressions and feelings of the young priest ('C'est elle [...] il espère'). A second feature is that the meeting is dramatized and mildly eroticized. The protagonists are placed before the reader in an enclosed setting ('n'ayant pour témoins que ces murs, que ces voûtes'). And their encounter is evoked economically by a short sequence of auditory, visual, and tactile impressions: 'murmurent à voix basse, et leurs bouches s'approchent, leur souffle se confond'. Such sensuousness, though restrained, is striking because it is most unusual in Courier. And finally, the persuasive impact is enhanced by rhetorical questions: 'que se passe-t-il dans l'âme?'; 'que vous semble?'; 'ils causent; de quoi?' These questions focus the narrative relentlessly on the issue in hand and exclude any suggestion that this is mere eroticism for its own sake.

Courier then resists advocates of religious revival who considered Christianity the foundation of morality and all social order, while also condemning the Church's attempts to bring about revival by coercion. The second *Réponse*, moreover, illustrates the possibility of dramatic divergence between the morality of Courier's Golden Rule and some types of Christian piety. This divergence is important in principle, and in practice it is a major part of Courier's rejection of the Church's pretensions to uphold morality and simultaneously to subordinate morals to formal piety. Clearly, such views tend to reduce any justification for clerical intrusions in everyday life. Additionally, of course, the Church is accused of placing unbearable burdens on its priests and, when they err, of offering them refuge and specious defences rather than leaving them to the justice of men. Some of Courier's criticism is more or less traditional: depravity due to celibacy was an eighteenth-century subject (as in Diderot's *Religieuse*). But Courier was not simply repeating platitudes because, for him, the alleged dependence of morality on religion was a topical issue. And it must be underlined that he expresses personal sympathy for the priests' plight. Once again, we see the fair-mindedness which he showed as early as the Calabrian campaign. Of all institutions, however, the Church had by this time become Courier's main target. It was not unusual for liberals to be anti-clerical (as distinguished from anti-religious) but, as often, Courier's concerns were particularly pertinent to the everyday lives of the humble who were vulnerable to clerical meddling.

CHAPTER 5

Pamphlets, 1823–1824: The Spanish War and a Farewell

In 1823, Courier published the *Livret de Paul-Louis*, the *Gazette du Village* and the *Pièce diplomatique*, followed by the apparently valedictory *Pamphlet des pamphlets* of 1824. Along with recurrent topics, such as the corruption of the court or clerical influence, the first three texts have a new dimension, the Spanish crisis of 1822–3. This episode originated in 1808 when Napoleon replaced the Bourbon King Fernando VII of Spain with his brother Joseph, hitherto King of Naples. An independent Spanish government resisted Joseph and adopted its own Constitution in 1812. On regaining power in 1814, Fernando ignored the Constitution and began wholesale reaction. Chaos followed, and in December 1822 the Sainte Alliance decided to support Fernando by force, fearing that, if he were deposed again, the example might unsettle other kingdoms. The French government agreed to act for the Allies and successfully invaded Spain in April-May 1823. In France, however, the planned invasion had been contested on grounds of principle and also of prudence, for Napoleonic setbacks in the Peninsula showed that success was not guaranteed.

These debates are reflected in the *Livret* and the *Gazette*, set, respectively, in Paris and the countryside. The *Livret* centres largely on members of the social elite: typically, it opens with Talleyrand and Louis XVIII, and ends with the duc d'Angoulême, nominal commander of the French army in Spain (*OC*, 164, 174; *Éc*, 400, 409). The *Gazette*, meanwhile, evokes a rural world of men who, living by their own labour, may not all be poor, but are certainly not rich (*OC*, 176; *Éc*, 413). Both texts convey that, if the French army and other forces of reaction prevail in Spain, freedom in France may be lost. Obviously, Courier's earlier pamphlets had suggested repeatedly that liberty in France was limited and fragile. The *Livret* adds that the provinces are already in a state of subjection to Paris: 'toute affaire se décide à Paris; les provinces sont traitées comme pays conquis' (*OC*, 166; *Éc*, 402). This analogy recalls Courier's views on the repression of resistance in the Kingdom of Naples which, as we have seen, France governed as a 'pays ennemi occupé par les troupes de la république'. Though in France opponents of the government rarely risked death, as they often did in occupied Italy, the population as a whole certainly suffered from oppressive policing:

> La police est le plus puissant des moyens inventés pour rendre un peuple vil et lâche. Quel courage peut avoir l'homme élevé dans la peur des gendarmes, n'osant ni parler haut, ni bouger sans passeport, à qui tout est espion et qui craint que son ombre ne le prenne au collet? (*Livret*, *OC*, 167; *Éc*, 402)

The gendarme was an ominous figure as of the *Pétition aux deux Chambres*, but here and, as we shall see, especially in the *Gazette*, the police presence is more insidious and morally debilitating. Pervasive policing saps Frenchmen's will to defend their freedom.

The *Livret* suggests that royal policy towards Spain is being shaped initially by women who have the king's ear but is determined finally by priests. The ladies, including the Duchesse de Berry's 3-year-old daughter, favour peace: 'Mademoiselle, ayant consulté sa poupée, se déclare pour la paix.' But all in vain, for 'voici le temps de Pâques, et tous les confesseurs refusent l'absolution si on ne fait la guerre. Elle se fera donc' (*OC*, 172; *Éc*, 407). Caricatural as it is, this passage echoes the *Pétition pour des villageois* in criticizing intrusive priests, and the coercive use of confession, though now the issue is not dancing, but peace and war, a war intended, according to Courier, to restore the pre-Revolutionary order. Thus, a mock Proclamation tells the soldiers of the French expeditionary force for Spain: 'quand vous aurez rétabli l'ancien régime en ce pays-là, on vous ramènera ici pour en faire autant' (*Livret*, *OC*, 174; *Éc*, 398).

The *Livret* dramatizes the theme of freedom through the affair of the liberal député Jacques-Antoine Manuel. In the debate on funds for the invasion of Spain, he was amongst the most vehement critics, and was barred from the Chambre for his allegedly intemperate words. When he returned and refused to leave, the gendarmerie ejected him. Courier writes that Manuel's was 'le plus bel acte dont l'homme soit capable, résister au pouvoir. De pareils traits sont rares; il les faut recueillir et les représenter, les recommander au peuple.' The text adds that his stance was noble because he was relatively disinterested, unlike his supine, selfish opponents: 'ceux-ci servant des maîtres et calculant d'avance le profit, la récompense toujours proportionnée à l'infamie de l'action; celui-là se proposant l'approbation publique et la gloire à venir' (*OC*, 171; *Éc*, 406). Primarily, this contrast glorifies the heroic individual. The depiction of Manuel is somewhat akin to Courier's view of himself as an isolated critic of power, a role underlined in the *Avertissement sur la Lettre à M. Renouard*, and the *Pamphlet des pamphlets* (*OC*, 248, 219; *Éc*, 86, 460). The text may also owe something to the mood of the time, with its admiration 'for minorities as such, for defiance as such, for failure as being nobler in certain respects than success'.[1] However, in extolling Manuel's defiance as a model for the people, the text can also be taken to encourage resistance not only by lone heroes, but by the whole population.[2] And though the war in Spain is the immediate issue, Courier praises 'résister au pouvoir' in such general terms that this passage could have wider implications. In the *Pétition aux deux Chambres*, he stressed that the 'peuple' needed to be defended by fit laws; here, we have at least a hint that the people must see to its own defence against the government.

Courier reports rumours that the artist Horace Vernet will paint the Manuel incident, and he is referring to this possible picture when he talks of showing the episode as an example to the people. It would contrast with the models that are in fact offered by prints which are 'caricatures, toutes contre le peuple. On le représente grossier, débauché, crapuleux, semblable à la cour, mais en laid. Afin de le corrompre, on le peint corrompu' (*Livret*, *OC*, 165; *Éc*, 401). We return, then, to the risk of moral degradation of the people, first evoked in the *Simple Discours*. But here too Courier's views have evolved. The *Simple Discours* had predicted that the Court would

1 Isaiah Berlin, *The Roots of Romanticism*, ed. Henry Hardy (London: Chatto & Windus, 1999), 140; Constant; *Œuvres*, 1369.

2 Dejammet sees the Manuel passage and the Proclamation as real calls for popular disobedience (pp. 553–4).

corrupt the local peasants, but only as an accidental result of proximity. Now corrupting the people has allegedly become a policy:

> Corrompre le peuple est l'affaire, la grande affaire maintenant. A l'église et dans les écoles, on lui enseigne l'hypocrisie; au théâtre l'ancien régime et toutes ses ordures. On lui tient prêtes des maisons où il va pratiquer ces leçons. (*OC*, 166; *Éc*, 401)

The shift in Courier's views may come partly from the change of location to Paris with its many licensed brothels: 'à Paris seulement, en 1824, fonctionnaient sous patente délivrée par le préfet de police [...] 163 maisons de tolérance, c'est-à-dire 18 de moins qu'en 1945 dans tout le département de la Seine'.[3] Whether or not there was a policy of fostering immorality, the main point of the *Livret* remains that the public can be guided for good or ill, needs wholesome guidance, and can find it in examples such as Manuel's. Conversely, Courier is coming to believe, even more than in relation to Chambord, that work and self-interest alone do not always give the people moral fibre.

The *Gazette* shows the creeping effects of the war and more generally of growing oppression as felt in the countryside. Thus several paragraphs refer to conscription, government spies, or fugitive deserters (*OC*, 177–9, 181, 183; *Éc*, 414, 416, 417–18). Conscription was familiar, but not spies:

> On voit dans nos campagnes des gens qui, ne gagnant rien, dépensent gros, étrangers, inconnus [...] On appelle ces gens, à la ville, des mouchards; à l'armée, des espions; à la cour, des agents secrets; aux champs, ils n'ont point de nom encore, n'étant connus que depuis peu. (*OC*, 178; *Éc*, 414)

The spies may not yet be dangerous, as they are easy to recognize, but their presence is a further symptom of a spreading police state. The gendarmes, meanwhile, are fearsome enough to cause panic amongst the deserters hiding in the area. In the extreme case of Urbain Chevrier, panic induces suicide: 'À la rumeur que fit l'arrivée des gendarmes, lui, comme hors de sens et déjà se croyant pris, s'en va tête baissée se jeter dans son puits' (*OC*, 181; *Éc*, 418). Such is the peasant's fear of the gendarme.

3 Bertier, 243.

Alongside spies and gendarmes, another oppressor is of course the mayor. The point reappears in an imaginary letter from a victim to Courier's persona, Paul-Louis, the imaginary editor of the *Gazette* (*OC*, 187–9; *Éc*, 423–5). This editor's closing footnote suggests that despotic mayors are common:

> Tout Paris s'imagine qu'aux champs on vit heureux du lait de ses brebis, en les menant paître sous la garde, non des chiens seulement, mais des lois; par malheur, il n'y a de lois qu'à Paris. Il vaut mieux être là l'ennemi déclaré des ministres, des grands, qu'ici ne pas plaire à M. le maire. (*OC*, 189; *Éc*, 425)

The context gives this letter to the editor particular force, because a thread of violence runs through the *Gazette*. There are reports of peasant suicides, though only Chevrier's case is connected directly with oppression. There are various assaults, more or less dramatized. The mayor of Véretz insults and attacks the 82-year-old curé (*OC*, 184; *Éc*, 420). On the other side, Milon, one of those imprisoned for sedition in 1815, assails a royalist landowner and a gamekeeper, whom he takes to be a spy (*OC*, 179; *Éc*, 415). It is in this charged context that the fictional letter complains of oppression by the mayor. The imaginary letter-writer quotes an Italian, according to whom Italians have 'deux remèdes contre l'insolence de MM. les maires, l'un appelé *stilettata*, l'autre *schiopettata* (*OC*, 189; *Éc*, 424–5). In a lawless land, like the Kingdom of Naples as described in Courier's letters (e.g. 107 [29]), knife and gun may indeed be the people's defence against tyrannical mayors. And if 'il n'y a de lois qu'à Paris', then rural France is potentially as lawless as southern Italy. True, the imaginary letter-writer prefers flight to the Italian remedy: 'semblable recette chez nous n'étant point d'usage, il ne me reste qu'un parti, de [...] déloger sans bruit' (*OC*, 189; *Éc*, 425). However, by juxtaposing Italian solution and French problem, Courier hints that desperate Frenchmen, finding themselves in a quasi-Italian situation, may also resort to murder. The *Pétition aux deux Chambres* had mentioned arson and the resultant risk to life in Luynes, but here the threat is no longer of accidental homicide, but of deliberate killing. Meanwhile, pending possible use of knife and gun, the aggrieved, such as Milon, content themselves with fist and boot (*OC*, 179; *Éc*, 415).[4]

Another theme of the *Gazette* is taxation, which is marginally related to intrusive policing and arbitrary use of power. Our starting point here is the outlook of those whose views reportedly inform the *Gazette*,

> laboureurs, vignerons, bûcherons, scieurs de long et botteleurs de foin [...] incapables de feindre ou d'avoir d'autres vues que leur propre intérêt, qui, comme chacun sait, est celui de l'État; tranquilles sur le reste, et croyant qu'eux repus, tout le monde a dîné. (*OC*, 176; *Éc*, 413)

As we have seen, Courier thought that the pursuit of self-interest was conducive to order, though he may have become less convinced of its effectiveness. The idea which emerges most clearly here is that pursuit of self-interest promotes the wealth of all. In liberal circles, such views were current. According to the economist Jean-Baptiste Say, quoted in the *Censeur européen*, 'la richesse publique n'est que la réunion des richesses particulières'.[5] These countrymen live their lives according to a kind of untutored liberalism. As for taxation, French liberal theorists did not normally reject it entirely but stressed that it should be reduced to a minimum. Jean-Baptiste Say underlines that taxes can increase production costs, and hence prices, and so inhibit consumption and business, hence the need to 'renfermer l'impôt dans les limites au delà desquelles il produirait une diminution de la consommation'.[6] Courier's rustics think similarly, according to their own interests: they want the *droits réunis* abolished; more generally they want taxes to be kept low, and used exclusively for public purposes. They hope that 'quand Bonaparte revienda, ou son fils que voilà tantôt grand, il ôtera les droits réunis, et ne lèvera d'argent que ce qu'il en faudra pour les dépenses publiques' (*Gazette*, *OC*, 183; *Éc*, 420). This formulation may imply that their hope is illusory, for Bonaparte was dead and his son barely 12 years old. But it also suggests

4 The letter-writer's woes are a colourful version of Courier's own dealings with Debeaune, the mayor of Véretz. Cf. Letter 643 [*196*], *CG* III, 232.

5 *Censeur européen*, vol. 1, p. 200.

6 Say, Jean-Baptiste, *Cours complet d'économie politique pratique*, 7 vols (Paris: Rapilly, 1829), vol. 4, p. 172.

their desperation, as they look for help from an Emperor, who had come to be hated for excessive conscription and taxation, the latter including even the *droits réunis*, which he had reintroduced in 1804.[7]

Prior to these economic considerations, however, a major problem affects consent to taxation. As we noted briefly in the Introduction, and may recall here, the *Charte* recognizes the principle that there must be no taxation without consent:

> Art. 48 Aucun impôt ne peut être établi ni perçu, s'il n'a été consenti par les deux Chambres et sanctionné par le roi.
>
> Art. 49 L'impôt foncier n'est consenti que pour un an. Les impositions indirectes peuvent l'être pour plusieurs années.

But the application of the principle is defective: under the electoral laws of 1817 and 1820, the electorate was restricted to men paying a minimum of 300 francs in direct taxes.[8] It is thus unlikely that Courier's rustics had representatives in the legislature or any way of giving or withholding their consent to taxation. They were no doubt subject to indirect rather than direct taxes but, for them, such taxation was arbitrary, and they readily regarded it as theft by the state. Typically, the story of widow Raillard and her illicit wine sales concludes that 'La contrebande n'est point une chose qu'on blâme [...] Le gouvernement trompe, et qui le peut tromper est approuvé de tous' (*OC*, 184; *Éc*, 420).

The persona Paul-Louis is also concerned by taxes. Having enumerated the main imposts applying to the wine which he produces, he concludes that rapacious taxation absorbs the bulk of his earnings:

> Paul-Louis a dix arpents qu'il cultive et façonne de la sorte avec sa famille. Ces bonnes gens en tirent tous les ans, comme on voit, quinze cents francs, dont ils vivent, et treize mille francs pour la splendeur du trône. Ce sont les appointements du procureur du roi qui a mis en prison Paul-Louis, et l'y remettra pour avoir fait ce calcul. (*OC*, 181; *Éc*, 417)

7 Bertier, 11; Tulard, *Napoléon*, 414.
8 Bertier, 146, 170.

Here, some links between taxation and oppression are clear: Paul-Louis's arithmetic speaks for itself and such is the likely impact of these lines that he anticipates imprisonment as for the *Simple Discours*. Placed just before the letter to the editor of the *Gazette* is a related ANNONCE, in which Paul-Louis offers his property Beauregard for sale (*OC*, 185–7; *Éc*, 422–3). Though he does not explain overtly why he seeks to sell, the juxtaposition with the letter seems significant. Both Paul-Louis and the letter-writer are being driven out: the former by confiscatory taxation, the latter by the mayor's abuses of power. Also underlying this passage is uncertainty about the result of the war in Spain and the possible return of the *ancien régime* in France. Some, such as the mayor, are astute and unscrupulous enough to accommodate any result. He is a commoner occupying the estate of an *émigré*, the marquis de Chabrillant. A return of the *ancien régime* might force him to restore his estate to Chabrillant. But despite his interest in protecting the fruits of the Revolution, his activity as mayor is wholly reactionary. The reasoning which Paul-Louis attributes to him is as follows: if the reactionaries fail in Spain, the situation in France will be unchanged and he will retain possession of Chabrillant's estate; and if the reactionaries succeed, they may be grateful for his attitude and 'il pense mériter non seulement sa grâce [...] mais récompense, emploi, et peut-être, qui sait? quelque autre terre confisquée sur les libéraux quand ils seront émigrés' (*OC*, 185; *Éc*, 421). Paul-Louis's advertisement, vaunting the advantages of Beauregard, is an ironic counterpoint to the mayor's thinking. If the *ancien régime* returns, Beauregard will regain its pre-Revolutionary status as a *terre seigneuriale* with all the attendant privileges, such as exemption from taxation, to mention only the most pertinent in the context (*OC*, 186; *Éc*, 422). But, if the *ancien régime* is not restored, Beauregard will continue as now, and indeed grow in value (*OC*, 186–7; *Éc*, 422–3). However, that claim is ironic because, if the output of Beauregard rises in value, it will go on suffering the extortionate taxation described in paragraphs 13–16; fiscal relief could come only through reversion to the pre-Revolutionary order, which Paul-Louis would obviously abhor. Unlike the reactionary, cynical mayor, who can scheme his way out of potential difficulty, Paul-Louis is nearly as helpless as the anonymous letter-writer.

As regards their structure, these pamphlets consist of short discrete entries. This is slightly unusual for Courier, but not unprecedented, as the *Lettres particulières* are also fragmentary in a plausibly epistolary manner. In the present cases, the form matches other fictional conventions. The full title of the first work is *Livret de Paul-Louis, Vigneron, pendant son séjour à Paris, en mars 1823*. Here 'livret' seems to mean simply 'notebook', and the text looks like the record of a short visit during which the writer noted down, as they happened, impressions, gossip, news reports, and personal meetings, for instance: 'Un homme, que j'ai vu, arrive d'Amérique' (*OC*, 166; *Éc*, 401); 'On a vu cela dans les journaux de la semaine passée' (*OC*, 167; *Éc*, 402). But despite its dispersal, the text has underlying focus on two intertwined topics: the court, and the prospect of war in Spain. The war appears in the opening paragraph, recurs in references to the Manuel episode, and dominates the last five pages; the court occupies a full page (*OC*, 170–1; *Éc*, 405–6), and other paragraphs on the current court, nobles, and ministers are scattered round the *Livret*. One link between the two subjects is that many courtiers and nobles would profit from an invasion of Spain: 'les fournisseurs de l'armée sont tous bons gentilshommes et des premières familles' (*OC*, 171; *Éc*, 406). Another link is that, as we have seen, the chief advocates of war are the confessors who hold sway at Court (*OC*, 172; *Éc*, 407). Regarding the observer, the word 'vigneron' implies that he is a non-resident, but he is not presented as being an ignorant peasant; on the contrary, he seems familiar with the private doings of courtiers, such as Ravez and Hyde de Neuville (*OC*, 169; *Éc*, 404). The *Livret* gives a plausible impression of a visitor's chance observations, and has a refreshing air of spontaneity, but is highly fragmented, covering at least forty items in just over ten pages. Such fragmentation, without necessarily amplifying Courier's criticisms, may simply confuse the reader.

The *Gazette du Village* mimics a newspaper with content made up of short items. The title recalls that of the publication which was in effect the government's official voice, the *Moniteur universel ou Gazette nationale*. By 1823, the title had been shortened to *Moniteur universel*, but the old title would have remained familiar enough to suggest that the *Gazette du Village* is a rustic answer to the *Gazette nationale*. The first paragraph asserts that this is the writer's record of what he has heard country people say: 'Paul-Louis, quelque peu clerc, écoute leurs récits, recueille leurs propos, sentences, dits notables, qu'il couche par écrit, et en fait ces articles, sans y mettre du sien, sans y rien sous-entendre' (*OC*, 176; *Éc*, 413). The apparently disjointed succession of items in the *Gazette* helps underpin that assertion. And the phrase 'sans y mettre du sien' implies that the persona Paul-Louis is simply showing rural realities as his neighbours see them. But clearly Paul-Louis does add his own touches, as in his frequent use of irony. The second paragraph, for instance, uses the polite title 'monsieur' so insistently that it becomes sarcastic: 'Monsieur le maire a entendu la messe [...] monsieur le maire a travaillé avec monsieur le brigadier [...] ces messieurs ont expédié [...] un paquet pour monsieur le préfet' (*OC*, 176–7; *Éc*, 413). The paragraph seems also to parody the court circulars published in the *Moniteur*. For example, the issue dated 27 November 1822 reports that on the twenty-sixth:

> Ce matin à huit heures et demie, le Roi a travaillé avec M. le duc de Doudeauville, directeur général des postes. Après la messe, S. M. a admis à l'honneur de prêter serment entre ses mains, MM. les évêques de Limoges, de Nantes et d'Amiens. A une heure et demie, le Roi a travaillé avec M. le comte de Villèle, président du conseil des ministres. S. M. n'est pas sortie. S. A. R. MADAME est allée à Villeneuve L'Etang. Mme la duchesse de Berry est allée se promener au Jardin du Roi. Les Enfans de France sont allés à Bagatelle.

Despite an appearance of dispersal, the *Gazette* has a relatively tight structure, thanks to a three-man schema of parallels and contrasts between the mayor, Paul-Louis, and the fugitive writer of the letter to the editor. Broadly, its 33 paragraphs and the letter turn on two intertwined themes: agriculture (paragraphs 1, 4, 9, 14, 15, 19, 20, 21, 23); and oppression, chiefly by the mayor, but also by intrusive churchmen and tax-collectors (paragraphs 2, 5, 8, 10, 11, 13, 16, 17, 18, 24, 25, 28, 29, the *Lettre*). The tighter construction of the *Gazette* offers glimpses of existence in the country that are easier to grasp than the Parisian scenes in the *Livret*. Of the two essays in fragmentary writing, the *Gazette* seems more successful.

The last pamphlet overtly about Spain, the *Pièce diplomatique extraite des journaux anglais*, is a bogus letter from Louis XVIII commending the French form of government to Fernando VII. The title itself proves slightly comic because the letter is familiar rather than formally 'diplomatique'. Louis first asserts total belief in divine-right monarchy. He then spends five paragraphs boasting that he has coupled the reality of divine-right kingship with a semblance of representative government, and that the arrangement pays, for parliament approves lavish royal expenditure and commensurate taxation. Finally, he offers Fernando practical help and advice: to introduce the system, he can lend a minister and a score of prefects; his advice includes granting a *Charte Constitutionnelle* to pacify his opponents, and ennobling some to buy their acquiescence (*OC*, 193; *Éc*, 430). This fictitious letter thus combines several of Courier's familiar themes.

Much rests on Louis's supposed conception of monarchy. His first paragraph, lauding rule by divine right, ends resoundingly: 'Quoi qu'il puisse arriver, périssent les nations plutôt que le droit divin!' (*OC*, 191; *Éc*, 428). Elsewhere in Courier, the expression 'droit divin' is unusual, and 'l'absolu', which occurs in the next paragraph, is non-existent; the changed terminology helps to give the character Louis some individuality and also marks that here Courier's perspective on government is slightly new.[9] As generally used, the expression 'droit divin' is taken to mean that the king's authority comes from God, and that he answers only to God. Here, Louis gives the idea his own slant: he says nothing about answering to God, but stakes his honour on upholding 'droit divin', as he interprets it. His interpretation is that, internally, he should consider only the wishes of court and clerics while disdaining his other subjects: 'gouvernons à l'exemple de nos prédécesseurs, sans écouter jamais que nos valets, nos maîtresses, nos favoris, nos prêtres; c'est l'honneur de la couronne' (*OC*, 191; *Éc*, 428). Externally, he must bow to foreign powers because he lacks popular support at home:

> je serais le plus grand roi d'Europe, si j'eusse voulu seulement m'entendre avec mon peuple [...] Me préserve le ciel d'une telle bassesse! J'obéis au congrès, aux princes, aux cabinets, et en reçois des ordres souvent embarrassants, toujours fort insolents;

9 Three earlier occurrences of 'droit divin' refer ironically to the claims of parasitical nobles or courtiers (*LCens* IX, *OC*, 36; *Éc*, 210; *Discours*, *OC*, 86; *Éc*, 274; *Gazette*, *OC*, 183; *Éc*, 419); a fourth concerns Louis's alleged wish to reorder Spain 'selon le droit divin' (*Livret*, *OC*, 171; *Éc*, 406).

> j'obéis néanmoins. Mais ce que veut mon peuple, et que je lui promis, je n'en fais rien du tout, tant j'ai de fierté dans l'âme et d'orgueil de ma race. (*OC*, 190–1; *Éc*, 427–8)

The idea that the king was himself exploited by his courtiers and other parasites had already featured prominently, for instance, in *Aux âmes dévotes*. However, by linking Louis's contempt for the people with his weakness in dealing with parasites and foreign powers, Courier revitalizes his satire on Louis's kingship. Where his earlier texts had stigmatized courtiers more than the king, here Louis is mocked as a willing dupe, besotted with vanity and a twisted conception of divine-right monarchy.[10]

This view of 'droit divin' also has implications for the *Charte Constitutionnelle*. In his preamble, the real Louis had undertaken to observe its provisions:

> nous nous engageons, devant l'Assemblée qui nous écoute, à être fidèle à cette charte constitutionnelle, nous réservant d'en jurer le maintien avec une nouvelle solennité, devant les autels de celui qui pèse dans la même balance les Rois et les Nations.[11]

Louis's imaginary advice to Fernando assumes, however, that such undertakings are void: 'il ne faut jamais recevoir la loi des sujets, jamais composer avec eux, ou du moins nous croire engagés par de telles compositions, vaines et nulles de droit divin' (*OC*, 190; *Éc*, 427). These pompous pronouncements are part of Courier's caricature of Louis, but the words 'vaines et nulles de droit divin' also highlight a real question about the *Charte*: if the divinity has instituted the authority of the French monarchy, can an individual monarch curtail or renounce that authority for himself and all his successors? The traditional answer, settled as of the Middle Ages, was clearly 'No',[12] and in reality Louis's successors would have had good grounds to revoke the *Charte*. As for the real Louis himself, he could have been sincere in his undertakings, if he had been unaware

10 Rule by divine right need not be absolutist. On this point and the divine-right ruler's responsibility to God, see Nicholas Henshall, *The Myth of Absolutism* (Harlow: Longman, 1992), 142–3.

11 Rials, 49.

12 Oscar Ferreira, 'Le Roi "dans" la Charte de 1814. Prisons imaginaires', *Jus Politicum*, 13 (2014), 5.

that his *Charte* had this defect. But if he had been aware of the defect, his undertakings, like those of his caricatural counterpart, would have been cynical. The fictional Louis certainly conveys that the real Louis's *Charte* may well have been empty. The fictional Louis advises Fernando:

> Octroyez, mon Cousin, octroyez une Charte constitutionnelle et tout ce qui s'ensuit : droit d'élection, jury, liberté de la presse; accordez et ne vous embarrassez de rien [...] Quand vous aurez traité avec vos *Libérales* [...] et juré l'oubli du passé à tous ces révolutionnaires, faites-en pendre cinq ou six aussitôt après l'amnistie, et faites les autres ducs et pairs. (*OC*, 193; *Éc*, 430)

These lines sum up concisely our pamphleteer's disenchantment with the *Charte.*[13]

The parliamentary regime, according to Louis, exists to approve the budget, and is far more lucrative than absolutism: 'J'aime l'absolu; mais ceci ... pour le produit, ceci vaut mieux [...] Le représentatif me convient à merveille, pourvu toutefois que ce soit moi qui nomme les députés du peuple, comme nous l'avons établi en ce pays fort heureusement' (*OC*, 191; *Éc*, 428).[14] If falsifying elections does not produce a docile legislature, the Crown uses bribery. By Louis's standards, députés are cheap: 'cent voix ne me coûtent pas [...] chaque année un mois de Mme du Cayla'. Here we may add that, whereas Courier had occasionally criticized députés for being ineffectual, here the imaginary Louis highlights their venality. Regarding Louis's use of the funds voted by parliament, the *Pièce* highlights one new point, namely that they pay for repression.[15] He recalls that he has plenty of money 'pour les Souverains étrangers, qui m'empêchent de recevoir la loi de mon peuple' (*OC*, 192–3; *Éc*, 429). The fictitious letter conveys succinctly that the parliamentary regime is false, the selfishness

13 The *Avertissement du Libraire* (1823), a bogus catalogue of Courier's forthcoming works, includes an *Autopsie du cadavre de la défunte Charte* (*OC*, 195; *Éc*, 465).

14 After losing an election to the marquis d'Effiat, Courier wrote that he had been cheated and that, morally, he was 'l'élu du département [...] M. le marquis est l'élu des ministres' (*Lettre au rédacteur du 'Drapeau Blanc'*, *OC*, 197; *Éc*, 337).

15 Under the peace treaty of 1815, France met the costs of the Allied occupation (Bertier, 130).

of parliamentarians real. By implication, Courier is as disabused with the legislature as with the *Charte*.

What adds yet further spice to these and other implicit criticisms in the *Pièce* is the depiction of Courier's unwitting spokesman, the fictional Louis XVIII. He lets himself be exploited by his entourage and humiliated by foreign rulers; in order to enrich himself and keep power, he uses dishonourable means. With such features, he could appear odious, but the character depicted here has a more likeable characteristic, his quest for amusement. Parliament, for instance, provides diversion as well as money. Thanks to the députés' petty greed,

> Vous aurez [...] le passetemps de leurs débats, chose la plus drôle du monde, vrai tapage de chiens et de chats qui se battent dans la rue pour des bribes. Quand leurs criailleries deviennent incommodes, on y fait jeter quelques seaux d'eau dès que le budget est voté. (*OC*, 193; *Éc*, 430)

Similarly, one reason for creating new nobles is to enjoy their crass attempts to merge with the old nobility: 'ne manquez pas d'y fourrer une nouvelle noblesse que vous mêlerez avec l'ancienne, autre espèce d'amusement qui vous tiendra en bonne humeur et en santé longtemps. Sans cela, aux Tuileries, nous péririons d'ennui' (ibid.). Such lines obviously convey Louis's disdain for the new nobility but also, more appealingly, his lucidity about the tedium of his own court.

In the comic portrayal of Louis, however, his attitude to Fernando may be more important. Implicitly, he justifies his offer of advice by greater experience: 'Je pensais comme vous vraiment avant mon voyage d'Angleterre; je n'aimais pas du tout ce représentatif; mais là j'ai vu ce que c'est' (*OC*, 191; *Éc*, 428). The letter does not present advice neutrally, but seems designed to persuade. In his own apologia for divine-right monarchy, Louis suggests that he is simply agreeing with Fernando: 'j'entre, comme vous voyez, dans tous vos sentiments, et prie Dieu qu'il vous y maintienne' (ibid.). This is of course flattery to make the reactionary Spanish king more receptive, for Louis adds at once: 'mais je ne puis approuver de même votre répugnance pour ce genre de gouvernement [...] représentatif' (ibid.). From tact and polite phraseology, Louis slips into condescension and an informal style. An example amongst many is this contrast between absolutism and representative government as sources of revenue: 'vantez-moi votre absolu, qui produisait à feu mon frère, quoi? trois ou quatre cents millions par an, avec combien de peine! Ici, chaque budget un milliard, sans la moindre difficulté' (*OC*, 192; *Éc*, 429). Its mockingly direct imperative ('vantez-moi') and equally mocking possessive 'votre' associate Fernando with a system which produces sums that are almost too small for Louis to count. This is all very dismissive.

At the more technical, rhetorical level, Louis resorts to homely analogies, as when he likens representative government to a pressure-cooker: 'une comparaison va vous rendre cela sensible [...] la marmite à vapeur, qui donne chaque minute un potage gras lorsqu'on la sait gouverner [...] voilà mon représentatif' (ibid.). Pursuing the homely parallel, he cajoles Fernando in even more familiar terms: 'Allons, mettez de côté vos petites répugnances et faites potage avec nous en famille' (ibid.). In the end, he treats Fernando like a child, as when he dismisses fears of a parliamentary system: 'Le budget suffit à tout, et voilà ce que c'est que ce représentatif dont là-bas vous vous faites une peur. Sottise, enfance, mon Cousin; il n'est rien de meilleur au monde' (*OC*, 193; *Éc*, 430). These elementary, domestic analogies suggest that Louis thinks Fernando singularly stupid.

Another notable feature of Louis's didactic manner is the rhetorical figure metanoia (or correction), which replaces a first term or expression with a second and so highlights the second, for example, 'ce genre de gouvernement qu'on a nommé représentatif, et que j'appelle, moi, récréatif'(*OC*, 191; *Éc*, 428) He says likewise of his plethoric budget: 'nous comptons ici par milliards, ou, pour dire la vérité, [...] nous ne comptons plus' (ibid.). But this same device produces comic bathos, as when Louis boasts that representative government places no restrictions on his use of funds: 'nous n'en faisons pas moins tout ce que nous voulons, c'est-à-dire ce que veulent nos courtisans' (ibid.). As corrected, his boast is an implicit admission that he is simply a puppet.

In summary, Louis is comically disdainful, and his disdain gives added bite to attacks on targets which Courier had attacked in his own name, such as voracious courtiers and ineffectual parliamentarians. Louis is also himself manipulated, which echoes Courier's earlier pamphlets; but here the manipulation, contrasting with Louis's sense of superiority, gives added comic force to the portrayal of the king. Finally, the sense that Louis finds the situation amusing gives him a certain endearing humanity. This is one of Courier's most appealing pamphlets because it depicts his enemy, not simply as a tyrant or a fool, but also as a human being with a capacity for fun.[16] As for Courier the writer, this scintillating piece demonstrates indisputably his continuing capacity for self-renewal.

The *Pamphlet des pamphlets*, giving some of Courier's general views on the genre, may serve as an epilogue. Amongst Courier's pamphlets, this text is unusually formal in structure: it reports criticism of pamphlets, praise of pamphlets, and finally gives the writer's own conclusions. The criticism echoes his trial for the *Simple Discours*, while the praise is ascribed to an imaginary British correspondent, Sir John Bickerstaff.[17] Essentially, the text turns on the contrast between France and the United States. The French establishment, embodied in de Broë and Bertrand, described as a juror at the *Simple Discours* trial, thinks all pamphlets evil. According to the *Pamphlet*, to have Courier convicted, de Broë had needed only to call him in court a 'vil pamphlétaire': 'soulevant contre moi les juges, les témoins, les jurés, l'assemblée (mon avocat lui-même en parut ébranlé), ce mot décida tout' (*OC*, 209; *Éc*, 451). Though de Broë may not have said literally 'vil pamphlétaire', he certainly accused pamphleteers of bias. Courier's pages on the immorality of François Ier and of Louis XIV led him to contrast the historian with the 'pamphlétaire' or 'libelliste': impartiality is the historian's duty, but the 'libelliste [...] ne présente jamais, d'un tableau historique, que le côté qui convient au parti dont il est le champion'.[18] And Bertrand thinks that 'Qui dit pamphlet, dit un écrit tout plein de poison' (*OC*, 210; *Éc*, 452). For such critics, the words 'pamphlet' and 'pamphlétaire' are pejorative, not mere technical terms referring to a short publication. Bertrand does not say what he means by 'plein de poison' – wisely, since he seems not to read any pamphlets for himself. If he believes that a given work is

16 According to Stendhal, the text delighted readers (*Courrier anglais* I, 153, quoted in Dejammet, 601).

17 Crouzet associates the name, plausibly, with the verb 'to bicker' (*Éc*, 461, n. 9). According to a letter to his friend Dalayrac, Courier studied English before a possible French incursion in Ireland (41 [11], 5 September 1798, *CG* I, 98).

18 *Moniteur universel*, 29 August 1821, p. 4.

'poisonous', it is because the authorities say so: 'publiez tout ce que vous voudrez, mais non pas du poison [...] le gouvernement est là qui vous en empêchera bien' (*OC*, 211; *Éc*, 452). Though uncritical in accepting official judgements, Bertrand does raise a potentially valid point about short works, namely that they must be over-simplified: 'que voulez-vous mettre de bon sens en une misérable feuille? Quelles idées s'y peuvent développer? Dans des ouvrages raisonnés, au sixième volume à peine entrevoit-on où l'auteur en veut venir' (*OC*, 211; *Éc*, 452–3). His preference also suggests an unspoken anxiety: criticism of the authorities will be safely buried in the multi-volume work that he favours but will stand out in a pamphlet. Obviously, if juries are composed of such uncritical government supporters as Bertrand, dissident pamphleteers will find them unsympathetic. The point is underlined by Courier's second trial when, with no jury, the magistrates acquitted him. But the example of Bertrand is crucial here because it highlights an even more fundamental reality: in France, the impact of criticism is muted, not only by authoritarian governments but also by public opinion – meaning the opinion of the propertied classes.

The most distinctive pages are Bickerstaff's praise of American pamphlets and newspapers. His starting point is the publication of *Common Sense* in 1776, when the colonies were debating secession from Britain:

> Franklin [...] vit son pays libre, ayant plus que nul autre aidé à l'affranchir par son fameux *Bon Sens*, brochure de deux feuilles. Jamais livre ni gros volume ne fit tant pour le genre humain [...] On vit [...] ce que peut la parole écrite dans un pays où tout le monde lit, puissance nouvelle et bien autre que celle de la tribune. (*OC*, 216; *Éc*, 457)

Common Sense was of course written by Tom Paine not Franklin, and the original, running in fact to 47 pages, was slightly more than a 'brochure de deux feuilles' (32 pages in-8°). In attributing these lapses to Bickerstaff, the *Pamphlet* conveys that he is fallible, and that his praise of America need not be wholly reliable. With that proviso, however, his claims about the United States are arresting. The press is free: 'Là tout s'imprime; rien n'est secret de ce qui importe à chacun' (*OC*, 217; *Éc*, 457–8). Because Americans prefer newspapers and pamphlets to books, there is a speedy flow of publications, which allows timely exchange of information and argument. Hence public opinion is, so to speak, self-correcting: 'Nos

Américains ne publient guère leurs idées que [...] dans les pamphlets, les journaux qui, se corrigeant l'un l'autre, amènent toute invention, toute pensée nouvelle à sa perfection' (*OC*, 217; *Éc*, 458). The process depends also on the literacy of the Americans, 'le seul peuple qui lise', according to Bickerstaff, and on their constructive approach: 'tout le monde presque écrit dans les journaux, mais sans légèreté; [...] l'expression claire et nette suffit à ces gens-là' (ibid.). Thanks to such debate of public affairs, 'La nation, comme si elle était toujours assemblée, recueille des voix et ne cesse de délibérer sur chaque point d'intérêt commun, et forme ses résolutions de l'opinion qui prévaut dans le peuple tout entier' (*OC*, 218; *Éc*, 459). Though some terms are unclear, the 'nation' seems here to mean the government of the USA, guided by public opinion, which is itself well informed and shaped by free discussion.[19] Unsurprisingly, Bickerstaff contrasts the USA and France: 'La presse n'y fait nul mal, et en empêche ... combien? C'est à vous de le dire, quand vous aurez compté chez vous tous les abus' (*OC*, 217; *Éc*, 458).

Bickerstaff's praise of press freedom reflects a common view amongst French liberals: 'D'un point de vue libéral classique, c'est la rencontre et le frottement des opinions individuelles qui engendre [sic] l'opinion publique.'[20] Such is the basis, for example, of Constant's arguments against press censorship in his work, *De la liberté des brochures, des pamphlets et des journaux* (1814). His model is Britain where, he writes, bills are freely debated in print and, as a result, the legislators produce statutes more acceptable to the informed public:

> ils apprennent comment la majorité qui écrit et qui parle considère la loi qu'ils vont faire [...] Ils sont instruits de ce qui convient à la disposition générale; et l'accord des

19 Bickerstaff's USA was idealized, but not a fantasy. Alexis de Tocqueville takes a cautiously positive view of the American press in *De la démocratie en Amérique*, ed. André Jardin, 2 vols (Paris: Gallimard, 1986), vol. 1, Part ii, ch. 3, 'De la liberté de la presse aux États-Unis', pp. 275–86.

20 Lucien Jaume, 'La Conception doctrinaire de la liberté de la presse: 1814–1819', *Colloque Val Richer* (1993), 111–23 (p. 118). But some major French liberals, such as François Guizot, held a less libertarian view of public opinion. See Arthur Ghins, 'Benjamin Constant and Public Opinion in Post-Revolutionary France', *History of Political Thought*, 40/3 (2019), 484–514.

> lois avec cette disposition compose leur perfection relative, souvent plus essentielle à atteindre que leur perfection absolue.[21]

Courier's aspirations were akin to Bickerstaff's vision. He too desired press freedom, and he would have wanted public opinion to influence the executive. He deplored the lack of rational debate and, in particular, governments' reluctance to discuss any issue or even explain their own stance: regarding his criticisms of the Chambord purchase, for example, 'ils ne répondent mot, et me mettent en prison' (*Rép.* (1), *OC*, 148; *Éc*, 377). Conversely, in the ironic *Lettre IX au 'Censeur'*, the imaginary courtier complains that the invention of printing and especially of newspapers is taking power from the government: 'Si cet abus continuait [...] La nation enfin ferait marcher le gouvernement, comme un cocher qu'on paie, et qui doit nous mener, non où il veut ni comme il veut, mais où nous prétendons aller, et par le chemin qui nous convient; chose horrible à penser' (*OC*, 36; *Éc*, 210). On no normal definition of 'nation' could this happen in France, where the electorate was narrowly based on property, literacy was rare, and newspapers were expensive and often censored.[22] The fantasy of the French 'nation' directing the executive reflects, above all, paranoia in Courier's courtier and, more broadly, amongst the privileged in France. By transposing to the USA a vision of government guided by public opinion, the *Pamphlet* shows how far France was from such a situation.

As to Sir John's belief that free debate would automatically produce healthy opinion, Courier probably had doubts, for he saw that debate is often shaped by considerations of personal advantage, not of the common good. Thus, in the first *Réponse aux anonymes*, he writes: 'aisément je me range [...] à l'avis de ceux qui me parlent, pourvu qu'ils aient un avis et non de simples intérêts sur ces grandes questions débattues de nos jours' (*OC*, 147–8; *Éc*, 377). The meeting of press and public opinion also has more

21 Constant, *De la Liberté des brochures, des pamphlets et des journaux*, in *Œuvres*, 1223.

22 Newspapers were sold by subscription. It is estimated that in 1826 one Frenchman in 427 was a subscriber, but there would have been more readers, thanks to reading rooms with quite cheap membership (Bertier, 294).

perverse possibilities, such as libel. Sir John claims that, if all can publish, public debate corrects inaccuracies:

> La presse est plus libre que la parole ailleurs et l'on en abuse moins. Pourquoi ? C'est qu'on en use sans nul empêchement, et qu'une fausseté, de quelque part qu'elle vienne, est bientôt démentie par les intéressés que rien n'oblige à se taire. (*OC*, 217; *Éc*, 458)

However, Courier's own experience was that victims of calumny could be forbidden to answer, as in his controversy with Del Furia (*AvertRen*, *OC*, 245–6; *Éc*, 82–4.). A more insidious threat arises if the executive controls some newspapers and can censor the rest. The first *Réponse aux anonymes* claims that ministers, to discredit opponents, can falsify reports of trials:

> mes ennemis pourront, s'ils le jugent à propos, imprimer ma défense dans des feuilles à eux, me faire dire cent sottises […] à moi, à mes amis, défendu d'en dire mot, de réfuter, de démentir en aucune façon les réponses absurdes et les impertinences qu'il leur aura plu de m'attribuer. (*OC*, 151; *Éc*, 380)

Courier's distrust is shared by Constant, who argued during a parliamentary debate on press censorship (28 March 1820) that those who considered themselves to have been libelled should have a right to reply. Constant too underlined that ministers could appoint their own men as censors, libel their opponents in articles which the tame censors would approve, and then have the censors forbid publication of the victims' answers.[23] It was already clear, then, how easily the authorities could allow or cause the press to destroy an opponent's reputation. Libel worried the liberal elite more than the *peuple*, whose woes were Courier's more usual concern, but obviously he saw libel as a direct threat to himself. More broadly, he seems to have become wary of the new force of the press, which could do good, but could also do ill, depending on who controlled or used it.

Though interested mostly in the USA, Bickerstaff recalls one successful series of French pamphlets, Pascal's *Provinciales* against the Jesuits (*OC*, 215; *Éc*, 456). Though the example dates from the seventeenth century, it is still apt for the 1820s, when Courier feared a Jesuit resurgence after

23 *Discours*, vol. 1, pp. 257–8.

French intervention in Spain (*Gazette*, *OC*, 179; *Éc*, 415). Given the potential impact of a pamphlet, even in France, Sir John argues that anyone with anything to say in the general interest has a duty to publish:

> laissez-vous pendre, mais publiez votre pensée. Ce n'est pas un droit, c'est un devoir, étroite obligation de quiconque a une pensée, de la publier et mettre au jour pour le bien commun. La vérité est toute à tous. Ce que vous connaissez utile, bon à savoir pour un chacun, vous ne le pouvez taire en conscience. (*OC*, 214; *Éc*, 455)

Hitherto, Courier's ideas had centred on the author's right to publish (e.g. in *Lettres IX-X au 'Censeur'*). In placing the emphasis rather on the author's duty to publish, the text indicates a major change. Bichkerstaff urges Courier, 'qui seul en ton pays consens à être homme du peuple, ose encore être pamphlétaire' (*OC*, 219; *Éc*, 460). Such daring, he adds, brings persecution, and persecution spreads the truth:

> il faut cette aide, et tu ne ferais rien sans M. de Broë. C'est à toi de parler et à lui de montrer, par son réquisitoire, la vérité de tes paroles. Vous entendant ainsi et secondant l'un l'autre, comme Socrate et Anytus, vous pouvez convertir le monde. (*OC*, 219–20; *Éc*, 460)

This exhortation to publish the truth, also implies that prosecutions are futile and apt to produce effects contrary to those intended by the authorities. No doubt this is also the underlying reason for the dissuasive advice given to Courier by a nameless figure at the Préfecture de police in Paris: 'employez votre grand génie à faire autre chose que des pamphlets' (*OC*, 209; *Éc*, 451). The authorities do not positively wish to prosecute critics; they would prefer them simply to remain silent.

In his tentative conclusions, Courier rejects Bickerstaff's idea that in France he could be a modern Socrates: 'J'ai peur qu'il ne s'abuse, me croyant fait pour imiter Socrate jusqu'au bout' (*OC*, 220; *Éc*, 461). Certainly, Courier claimed elsewhere to have spoken out alone: 'seul, au temps de 1815, je rompis le silence de la France opprimée'.[24] But he maintains that his involvement is no longer needed: 'le monde de soi se convertit assez sans

24 *A MM. du Conseil de Préfecture* (1820), *OC*, 50; *Éc*, 230. However, Courier's criticisms of Napoleon before the Empire collapsed were mainly private, and he was not the only critic. Chateaubriand published implicit opposition as early as an article in the *Mercure* of 4 July 1807 (Lentz, *Napoléon: Dictionnaire historique*, 192).

que je m'en mêle, chétif. Je serais la mouche du coche, qui se passera bien de mon bourdonnement'. And he ends by saying of the 'coach', 'si sa marche nous paraît lente, c'est que nous vivons un instant. Mais que de chemin il a fait depuis cinq ou six siècles! A cette heure, en plaine roulant, rien ne le peut plus arrêter' (*OC*, 220; *Éc*, 461). Courier's idea that progress, though slow, is now unstoppable, diverges from the fear of counter-revolution apparent the previous year in the *Livret* and the *Gazette du village*. However, though irony is always possible in Courier, this muted optimism sounds real enough: it is consistent with his various earlier references to the peasants' material progress, and here it flows from an orderly review of the situation, delivered in a detached tone. Such thinking is more or less in keeping with the contemporary liberal view that society evolves, and that its evolution is progressive. However, many liberals accepted, like Courier, that progress was slow. Thus, for Say, in 1829, 'Les améliorations possibles sont immenses, celles qui s'opèrent réellement sont lentes et bornées; mais l'avenir est pour nous.'[25] The *Pamphlet des pamphlets* reads as if it were Courier's last word and, whatever his intentions, his murder made it so.

25 Say, *Cours complet d'économie politique pratique*, vol. 4, p. 452. Cf. Weinburg, 59.

CHAPTER 6

Aspects of Manner: Simplicity and Irony

Courier's manner varies between texts. In previous chapters, we have considered some of his expressive strategies as they appear in particular works. The object of this chapter is to review two significant, recurrent features of his manner, his alleged simplicity, and his irony.

Simplicity

Courier claims to have written, at least sometimes, in a conversational manner, as when he says that the *Pétition aux deux Chambres* was 'seize pages d'un style à peu près comme je vous parle' (*Pamphlet*, *OC*, 213; *Éc*, 454). Since informal conversation often rambles repetitiously, his remark should not be taken literally, but rather as implying concision, simplicity, and clarity; thus he adds that, in the *Simple Discours*, he had tried to express his ideas 'en peu de mots, sans ambages ni circonlocutions' (ibid.). He contrasts this style with the expansiveness of a writer such as Lamennais. The subject matter of the *Pétition* could, he asserts, have been treated much more rhetorically and developed indefinitely: 'si j'eusse commencé: *Chrétiens, après les attentats inouïs d'une infernale Révolution* … dans le goût de l'abbé de La Mennais, une fois monté à ce ton, il m'était aisé de continuer et mener à fin mon volume' (ibid.) He claims however to have been incapable of writing so copiously: 'la matière était ample à fournir des volumes et je n'en sus tirer qu'une feuille, tant l'éloquence me manqua' (*OC*, 212–13; *Éc*, 454). Nonetheless, his early *Éloge de Buffon* shows that he could in fact write expansively.[1] His main point, in stressing

1 For example, in a fourteen-line sentence on Buffon's *opus* as a whole: 'Si je m'attachais à dépeindre ce magnifique monument […] en donner un système complet' (*OC*, 559–60).

his own concision, is rather to disavow the oratorical manner, while accusing oratorical writers of mere facility, and their readers of preferring verbal abundance to meaningful content.

Courier's plain style has various notable aspects. One is simple sentence-structure, as exemplified in the Proclamation appended to the *Livret* and ostensibly addressed to French troops about to invade Spain in 1823. The text begins:

> Soldats, vous allez rétablir en Espagne l'ancien régime et défaire la révolution; ils ont détruit l'ancien régime, et à cause de cela on vous envoie contre eux; et quand vous aurez rétabli l'ancien régime en ce pays-là, on vous ramènera ici pour en faire autant. Or, l'ancien régime, savez-vous ce que c'est mes amis? C'est, pour le peuple, des impôts; pour les soldats, c'est du pain noir et des coups de bâton. (*OC*, 174; *Éc*, 398)

Independent clauses predominate, and the only subordinates are the adverb clause 'quand vous aurez …' and the indirect question '[savez-vous] ce que c'est'. The component clauses of the opening sentences are linked grammatically by coordination, with three 'et'. The sentences defining the *ancien régime* ('C'est, pour le peuple …') are paratactic, not linked syntactically. The sense is clear, being emphasized by repetition of 'ancien régime' with the accompanying antitheses *défaire/détruire* vs *rétablir* and the reductive definitions, 'des impôts', 'du pain noir et des coups de bâton'. If freedom from circumlocution is a virtue, this passage is certainly virtuous. The lines suit the supposed audience, one composed of largely uneducated soldiers. Elsewhere, a simple structure may have a narrative function, and relate rather to content than to the audience. A possible example is the story of a quarrel about seating in church in Tours:

> A l'église c'était grande cérémonie, office pontifical, cierges allumés, faux bourdon, procession, cloches en branle; le concours des fidèles et cet ordre pompeux faisaient plaisir à voir. Au beau milieu du chœur, deux champions couverts d'or se gourment, s'apostrophent. Ote-toi. – Non, c'est ma place. – C'est la mienne. – Tu mens. Coups de pied, coups de poing. (*Lpart* (1), *OC*, 59; *Éc*, 239)

The ceremony is evoked initially by a list of nouns or noun phrases ('office pontifical [...] cloches en branle'). The absence of verbs and qualifying adjectives hastens the report along, while conveying the assumption that the reader needs no further description of a celebration taking its usual form. Most unusual, by contrast, is the introduction of two contending 'champions couverts d'or', which readily catches the reader's attention. The 'concours des fidèles', initially for the religious ceremony, now becomes the audience for the confrontation 'au beau milieu du chœur'. The only verbs, 'se gourment, s'apostrophent', highlight the protagonists' arrogance and are, structurally, a turning point before the altercation in direct speech, and the brawl, which is condensed into a few nouns, 'Coups de pied, coups de poing'. The comic fall from 'grande cérémonie' to fisticuffs is swift, thanks in part to the compressed, paratactic structures.[2] The narration with a minimum of background information maintains the reader's curiosity about the identity of the gilded 'champions'. When the bishop's subsequent pleas for calm identify them, respectively, as the commanders of the regular garrison and the garde nationale, we readily accept the information, for the *Lettre* has already reported a clash in Saumur between the two corps (*OC*, 55–6; *Éc*, 236). Comical as it is, this narrative helps confirm most economically a major point of the *Lettre*, the disunity of the forces available to the government.

The type of vocabulary is another important aspect of the non-oratorical style. In general, Courier seems to prefer everyday words to terms with loftier connotations: the *Simple Discours* mocks, for instance, those 'qui ne peuvent souffrir qu'on dise mon champ, ma maison; qui veulent que tout soit terre, parc, château' (*OC*, 79; *Éc*, 268). Preference for plain language can thus be part of a satire on pretension. This is particularly evident in Courier's application of the principle of decorum, the principle that the style must fit the speaker and the subject. Several examples occur in the *Simple Discours*, in which the writer, 'vigneron de la Chavonnière', purports to address some peasants, in language appropriate to speaker and

2 This brisk narrative style also appears, for example, in the meeting of Fouquet and the priest in the *Pétition aux deux Chambres* (*OC*, 3; *Éc*, 124) or Courier's dealings with the prosecutors (*Lettre au 'Constitutionnel'*, 14 October 1823, *OC*, 203–4; *Éc*, 438).

audience. In the second paragraph, he says of the infant Duke: 'son métier, c'est de régner un jour' (*OC*, 72; *Éc*, 262). Later, contrasting the baby with Maurice de Saxe, whose military services had been rewarded, on his retirement, with the gift of Chambord, Courier writes: 'de Maurice vainqueur au prince à la bavette, il y a quelque différence' and he objects to the child's having 'ses invalides avant de sortir du maillot' (*OC*, 75; *Éc*, 264). At the trial, the prosecutor professed shock because

> l'auteur parle du jeune prince comme d'un enfant à la mamelle. Il dit le *maillot* simplement, sans dire *l'auguste maillot*; la *bavette* , et non pas la *royale bavette*. Il dit, chose horrible! de ce prince, qu'un jour *son métier sera de régner*. (*Procès*: *OC*, 99; *Éc*, 292)

Allegedly, then, Courier's language insults the grandeur of the future king. He retorts:

> dans ces paroles d'un paysan à un grand prince, *ton métier sera de régner* [...] ce mot vulgaire de *métier* relève, ennoblit l'expression, par cela même qu'il est vulgaire, tellement qu'elle ne serait pas déplacée dans [...] une ode à la louange du prince. Si on n'en saurait dire autant des autres termes employés par l'auteur dans le même endroit, ils ont tous du moins le ton de simplicité naïve, convenable au personnage qui parle. (*Procès*, *OC*, 104; *Éc*, 297)

Here, the principle of decorum is clearly a satirical weapon: the Duc de Bordeaux is indeed an 'enfant à la mamelle'; this banal reality is stated in plain terms by a supposedly simple speaker. While the terms are, according to Courier, perfectly worthy, they remove the aura of majesty that the court and establishment seek to impart.[3] Similarly, plain vocabulary, as used by Courier, expressly aims to exclude euphemism. (I stress 'as used by Courier' because in general a plain style does not in itself guarantee candour.) In the *Procès* he calls Gabrielle d'Estrées and her like 'prostituées', and their activity 'débauche'. But, he says, these blunt words offend 'la décence, le bon ton', which require the writer to use such

3 To enhance the child's prestige he was, for example, likened to Henri IV. See Waresquiel, 'Des nécessités de la mémoire politique: Le mythe d'Henri IV', in *Penser la Restauration*, 319–42 (pp. 334–41).

terms as 'aimable friponnerie, fine galanterie, coquetterie du beau monde' (*Procès*, *OC*, 130; *Éc*, 322).

Another aspect of the plain style is a relative (but not total) absence of metaphor, a figure of which Courier expresses general distrust. When Bertrand complains that pamphlets contain 'poison', Courier thinks: 'Dieu délivre-nous du malin et du langage figuré! Les médecins m'ont pensé tuer, voulant me *rafraîchir le sang*; celui-ci m'emprisonne de peur que je n'écrive du *poison*; [...] Jésus, mon Sauveur, sauvez-nous de la métaphore' (*Pamphlet*, *OC*, 211; *Éc*, 452). The first metaphor is a euphemism for bleeding, the second is dangerously imprecise and emotive. Courier himself professes to take literally the metaphor of controversial content as poison, and expands on it by an analogy. (Analogy is not figurative, because the similarities are presented as being real, not imagined.)

> Dans tout ce qui s'imprime, il y a du poison plus ou moins délayé selon l'étendue de l'ouvrage, plus ou moins malfaisant, mortel. De *l'acétate de morphine*, un grain dans une cuve se perd, n'est point senti, dans une tasse fait vomir, en une cuillerée tue, et voilà le pamphlet. (*OC*, 213; *Éc*, 454)

As Courier presents it here, metaphor reduces clarity and so works against a potential virtue of the plain style.

Yet despite his stated preference for plain language, his vocabulary is sometimes erudite. When he says that the *Simple Discours* was meant to be written 'sans ambages ni circonlocutions', that expression is itself learned. The corpus of nineteenth- and twentieth-century language examined by the *Trésor de la langue française* totals 48 instances of 'circonlocution', and 55 of 'ambages' – as against 1,757 occurrences of 'détour', though the comparison is imperfect, since 'détour' is not simply a synonym of 'circonlocution'. Use of these terms here serves no doubt to show that the writer is capable of such language and to underline that his preference for plain language is a matter of choice, not of ignorance. His vocabulary can also be technical as when, in his role as a wine producer, he talks of 'passer fleur', 'couler', and also employs a regionalism, 'lame' (*Gazette*, *OC*, 182; *Éc*, 419).[4] A comic example, in a passage already quoted, is the theological term 'ubiquité': 'le

4 *Éc*, 426, n. 7; *Trésor de la langue française*, s.v. lame.

gouvernement est partout aujourd'hui, et cette *ubiquité* s'étend jusqu'à nos danses' (*Villageois*, *OC*, 135; *Éc*, 344). Theologically, the word refers to God's presence in all places at all times.[5] Its application to the authorities' presence underlines their excessive pretensions, but also the disproportion between the power which they do have and the humble pastime to which it is being applied. Here, the technicality is highly satirical. These few examples tend to confirm that, objectively, the text does deploy some unusual vocabulary and they also suggest that the lexical rarities are, as a rule, used appositely. Erudite expression is not confined to individual terms but extends also to analogies and here, Courier's expression is sometimes less felicitous. An extreme example is his explanation of the illusion that the court, which morally is in fact beneath the nation as a whole, seems to be morally above. He explains this misperception by analogy with the physical refraction of light: 'le rayon visuel passant d'un milieu rare et pur, celui où nous vivons, dans un milieu plus dense, l'atmosphère dense et chargée de miasmes de la cour, nécessairement il y a réfraction; ce qui paraît dessus est en effet dessous' (*LCens* VIII, *OC*, 32; *Éc*, 205). This laborious account of an imaginary optical illusion shows that Courier committed occasional excesses of learning.

Another intriguing characteristic of his expression – not simply of his vocabulary – is the presence of archaisms or near-archaisms. The pamphlet *Aux âmes dévotes* is, we have suggested, reminiscent of Rabelais. It uses various terms which are not strictly archaisms, as they do occur in other nineteenth-century texts, but which are rare enough to cohere with the overall rabelaisian tone of the pamphlet. Examples include the following with, in parentheses, the numbers of occurrences recorded by the *Trésor*: 'engeance' (80); 'dilapidation' (32); 'flagornerie' (31); 'flagorneur' (25). For comparison with 'flagorneur', the *Trésor* counts 990 instances of 'flatteur'. More genuine archaisms appear in the claim that parasitical courtiers 'enlèvent du produit de nos champs [...] le plus beau, dont bien fâche audit seigneur roi' (*OC*, 88; *Éc*, 281). Here, the usage of the sixteenth century or earlier is reflected in 'dont' for 'ce dont', and in 'fâche' used impersonally

5 *Petit Robert*, s.v. 'ubiquité'.

with no subject pronoun.[6] Elsewhere, an amusing archaism concerns the rising status of peasants: 'Ces nouveautés choquent furieusement les propriétaires, j'entends ceux qui pour le devenir n'ont eu que la peine de naître' (*LCens* I, *OC*, 12; *Éc*, 183). The adverb 'furieusement', is notoriously associated with the *précieuses* of about 1660, and its presence here suggests that the old landowners' outlook belongs to the same period. The examples above seem to contribute to the impact of the text. And, though a full assessment of Courier's archaisms is beyond the scope of this book, these examples certainly confirm further that his expression is not confined to the everyday language of the early nineteenth century.

Finally, we may note that Courier's plain style did not totally exclude plays on sounds (e.g. assonance, alliteration) or on words (e.g. paronomasia). The most conspicuous examples of assonance and alliteration are in the comic lists of parasites which we have already noted in *Aux âmes dévotes*. As for pun or paronomasia, some of the most notable examples are in parallel constructions where one keyword changes, or where the word remains but in a different sense, thus transforming the whole expression. The first type appears in the confrontation in Saumur between noble officers and Constant: the officers 'mettent l'épée à la main. L'autre mit ses lunettes'. The verbal contrast between belligerence and deliberation produces a comic anticlimax at the officers' expense. This effect is underlined by the next exchange, which is similar in structure but implicitly involves two different senses of 'raison': 'Ils lui demandaient *raison*. Je vois bien, leur dit-il, que c'est ce qui vous manque' (*Lpart* (1), *OC*, 55; *Éc*, 236). In the *Procès*, opening the prosecution, Me de Broë 'prit la parole, ou, pour mieux dire, prit son papier, car il lisait' (*OC*, 96; *Éc*, 289). As noted earlier, these lines may echo *Gargantua* but, in any case, the contrast *parole/papier* introduces succinctly the laborious reading that is to follow. To recall finally a well-known example, the *Gazette* tells us how the outcome of war in Spain will affect freedom in France: 'selon la tournure que prendront les affaires, on élargira la prison ou les prisonniers' (*OC*, 178; *Éc*, 415). These

6 For 'dont' and impersonal verbs without 'il', see Maurice Grevisse, *Le Bon Usage*, 11th edn (Gembloux: Duculot, 1980), §§1184, 1395. On 'fâcher' as an impersonal verb, Georges Gougenheim, *Grammaire de la langue française du seizième siècle* (Lyons: Édition IAC, 1951), 125.

few cases are perhaps enough to suggest that wordplay in these texts can serve to produce pertinent comic effects economically.

Irony

Irony, of which we have encountered many examples, is so prominent in Courier's writing that a brief synthesis may be helpful. In general, irony is multifarious in its nature and possible functions: for example, D. C. Muecke's guide identifies some 15 types.[7] However, for our purposes, we have taken the basic view that irony has three components: a surface meaning, a divergent underlying meaning, and some hint that the latter has precedence. Here we may add the distinction between 'instrumental' and 'observable' irony. The distinction is familiar, but the definition of the two categories is slightly uncertain. As used here, the term 'instrumental' designates irony which emanates unequivocally from the writer or speaker, and usually applies directly to his target. In Courier's practice, it is most apparent when the underlying meaning is the exact opposite of the surface meaning, a configuration sometimes termed 'antiphrasis'. Such instrumental irony quite often focuses on Napoleon Bonaparte. In observable irony the target – unwittingly – discredits himself by expressing views that plainly conflict with common sense or some other recognizable standard. In such cases, the ironic writer simply presents the target for the reader to inspect: one such is the imaginary speaker in *Lettre IX au 'Censeur'* who, from prehistoric times, would have used total censorship to defend every privilege. The distinction between instrumental and observable irony is clear enough in principle and also quite helpful. However, in Courier there are also ironies with mixed characteristics, and care must be taken not to assign those cases arbitrarily to one category or the other. For example, one of Courier's imaginary neighbours subjects Lamennais to observable irony through an invented quotation: 'Le jour de la création, quel bruit n'eût-il pas fait ! il eût crié, Mon Dieu, conservons

7 D. C. Muecke, *Irony and the Ironic*, rev. edn (London: Methuen, 1982), 8–13.

le chaos' (*LCens V*, *OC*, 21; *Éc*, 193). It is observable that the victim condemns himself by the words attributed to him. But it is also instrumental in that it is part of an explicit, direct attack on Lamennais, and is explicitly invented by the neighbour. De Broë is the target of a similarly mixed irony. After his imprisonment for the *Simple Discours*, Courier refers to 'la liberté de la presse, dont nous jouissons, comme dit bien M. de Broë, dans toute son étendue' (*Rép.* (1), *OC*, 146; *Éc*, 375). The irony is observable, given Courier's conviction, which demonstrated how limited was the 'étendue' of press freedom. The irony is also instrumental, in that Courier attributes a statement to de Broë in order to ridicule him. (These words are not in de Broë's speech, as reported in the *Procès*.)

Turning to instrumental irony, particularly as centred on Napoleon Bonaparte, we find that the pamphlets and the relevant letters use the name 'Napoléon' at least 11 times. In six of these cases, he is termed 'le grand Napoléon' or 'Napoléon le grand', an irony inspired perhaps by official adoption in 1806 of the formula 'Napoléon le Grand'.[8] In another 11 cases at least, he is not always named but is unequivocally designated by the terms 'héros' or 'génie', with negative import.[9] Thus, we read that 'ce grand homme est là où son rare génie l'a conduit', viz, to defeat and exile. These

8 *AvertRen*; (*OC*, 245); *Acad* (*OC*, 280; *Éc*, 158); *LCens IV* (*OC*, 16; *Éc*, 188); *LCens VIII* (*OC*, 33; *Éc*, 205); *Rép* (1) (*OC*, 150; *Éc*, 379); *Lettre au rédacteur du 'Courrier français'*, 4 October 1823 (*OC*, 201; *Éc*, 435). On the formula 'Napoléon le Grand', see Philip Dwyer, *Citizen Emperor: Napoleon in Power, 1799–1815* (London: Bloomsbury, 2013), 211.

9 'avec le génie de l'empereur nous vaincrons toujours' (Letter 135 [38], *CG* I, 230); 'un aide de camp [...] portant dans sa poche le génie de l'empereur [...] La bataille gagnée c'eut été l'empereur, le génie' (Letter 140 [43], *CG* I, 239); 'ce génie qui inventa la grande guerre et la haute police' (*Chambres*, *OC*, 8; *Éc*, 129); 'Napoléon, génie, dieu tutélaire des races antiques et nouvelles' (*Acad*, *OC*, 274; *Éc*, 152); 'le caractère de ce héros, le génie du pouvoir, qui faisait en une heure une constitution' (*LCens IV*, *OC*, 16, *Éc*, 188); 'ce grand homme est là où son rare génie l'a conduit' (*LCens VI*, *OC*, 24; *Éc*, 197); 'ne comptant plus pour les défendre sur le génie de l'empereur' (*LCens X*, *OC*, 46; *Éc*, 220); 'ni héros ni péquins' (*LCens X*, *OC*, 47; *Éc*, 221); 'le héros parut et fit venir d'Allemagne des parents ou alliés de nos ennemis' (*Discours*, *OC*, 85; *Éc*, 273); 'Bonaparte surtout; ce héros [...] jamais ne nous leurra [...] d'aucune liberté' (*Rép* (1); *OC*, 150; *Éc*, 379); 'le héros nous fit rasseoir' (*Pamphlet*, *OC*, 208; *Éc*, 450).

ironies belittle not only Bonaparte but also, at least by implication, those who unreasonably admire or flatter him. Sometimes irony at the expense of sycophants is not only implicit and instrumental but observable. In the last case listed in the note, from the *Pamphlet des pamphlets*, the irony is instrumental when directed at Bonaparte,'le héros', but observable when a flatterer becomes the target. In this instance, some junior officers had been eating together when Bonaparte, now Consul, arrived unexpectedly. In the ensuing, stilted conversation about food, Bonaparte said that he ate artichokes with salt, inspiring a gross compliment from one of the juniors: 'Ah! général, répond celui qui s'appelait alors Savary, vous êtes un grand homme; vous êtes inimitable' (*Pamphlet*, *OC* 209; *Éc*, 450). And in naming the servile officer as Savary, Courier also conveys that Bonaparte was susceptible to such obsequiousness, for he later made Savary Duc de Rovigo.

Courier's observable irony generally involves more or less reactionary stances which are exhibited for ridicule. Near the end of his career, the *Pamphlet des pamphlets* mentions an extreme situation where such irony can arise. Bickerstaff urges Courier to publish more pamphlets and allow himself to be prosecuted again by de Broë: 'C'est à toi de parler et à lui de montrer, par son réquisitoire, la vérité de tes paroles' (*OC*, 220; *Éc*, 460). Courier expresses reluctance to attract fresh prosecutions (*OC*, 220; *Éc*, 461), but the advice attributed to Bickerstaff implies enduring faith in observable irony as a tool for the controversialist. In practice, the texts include many cases of observable irony, of which Lettre *IX* is perhaps the least subtle. As we know, the speaker holds that all expression must be stifled to protect the establishment. The very excesses of the views ascribed to the imaginary writer would suffice to tell us that the text is ironic, and any possible doubt about the subject (press censorship) and the target (the government) is removed by the second and third sentences: 'C'est la lettre moulée qui fait qu'on assassine depuis la création; et Caïn lisait les journaux dans le paradis terrestre. Il ne faut pas en douter; les ministres le disent, les ministres ne mentent pas' (*OC*, 34; *Éc*, 208).

The most accomplished example of observable irony is probably the *Pièce diplomatique*, the imaginary letter in which Louis XVIII commends parliamentary government to Fernando VII of Spain. Having already examined this text in Chapter 5, I need only add a remark on its quality as irony.

There is no external commentary, Louis simply expounds certain views. However, there is an implied dialogue with Fernando, as Louis sets about correcting the unthinkingly retrograde opinions for which Fernando was notorious. To a very limited extent, and by implication, the regime in Spain is a target: it is so flagrantly reactionary that even Louis can criticize it. But obviously the criticism falls chiefly on France, and includes, for example, the supine députés and the uncouth new nobles surrounding Louis. However, the main target of observable irony is Louis, who upholds both a degenerate form of absolutism that subordinates him to his own courtiers and also a corrupt form of representative government that represents no one, but gives him funds and amusement.

In certain cases of observable irony, Courier speaks through a persona of himself, as when he extols prosecutors (*LCens IV*, *OC*, 17; *Éc*, 189). Sometimes, other personae, imaginary neighbours, voice opinions consistent with Courier's usual views, while the persona of the author himself adopts retrograde postures as a vehicle for observable irony at the expense of reactionaries. Thus, the Courier persona rejoices that land will be taken from hard-working peasants and returned to its former owners, idle aristocrats, and churchmen (*LCensVI*, *OC*, 24; *Éc*, 196). This form of irony may risk confusion, perhaps particularly in *Lettre V*. The text is largely an imaginary neighbour's explicit defence of the *bandes noires*, a position which Courier was to uphold in his own name in the *Simple Discours*. In itself, the neighbour's argument is convincing enough, and not the target of irony. On the other hand, the opening and closing paragraphs, and also one interjection are attributed to the 'je' of the letter, the Courier persona who attacks the *bandes noires*, as do reactionaries hoping to stop or reverse the redistribution of land. There are small hints of observable irony in the first paragraph, for example, when 'je' rejoices that the *bandes noires* do not buy woodland, which is 'défendu par de vieilles lois, qui tiennent bon contre l'industrie' (*OC*, 18; *Éc*, 190). This expression overturns the usual positive connotations of 'industrie', meaning 'productive activity' and, ironically, makes the term pejorative.[10] Observable irony occurs more clearly in the last paragraph where 'je', rejecting his neighbour's praise of the

10 Positive connotations of 'industrie' appear in *LCens VIII* (*OC*, 31; *Éc*, 204); *Simple Discours* (*OC*, 83; *Éc*, 271). On surviving pre-Revolutionary regulation of

bandes noires, complains that, when peasants have land and feed themselves, 'la charité s'éteint, depuis qu'on songe à travailler, et se perdra enfin, si la Sainte-Alliance n'y met ordre' (*OC*, 22; *Éc*, 193). On this perverse view, the poor exist to let the rich practise charity and, to preserve this situation, the Allies must halt the *bandes noires* (ibid.). Readers familiar with Courier's usual support for smallholding will see the stance of 'je' as irony against unthinking reaction. However, anyone less familiar may simply be puzzled by the extreme priority that 'je' seems to give to charity.

A different case is the dialogue between Courier's persona Paul and his supposed acquaintance Cadet Roussel, the hero of the well-known song. Here, Paul does not contradict Courier's own opinion, but simply masks it and so leads Cadet himself to reveal the inconsistency of his ambitions. In this respect, the irony could almost be called 'Socratic'. Cadet has three houses, but they are better than those in the song:[11]

> l'une est celle de mon père, où je n'habite plus; l'autre appartenait ci-devant à M. le marquis de ... chose, qui s'en alla, je ne sais pourquoi, dans le temps de la révolution. J'achetai sa maison pendant qu'il voyageait. C'est celle où je demeure et me trouve fort bien. La troisième appartenait à Dieu, et de même je m'en suis accommodé. (*Lpart* (2), *OC*, 63; *Éc*, 244)

Like other buyers of *biens nationaux* Cadet fears that his may be compulsorily returned to their pre-revolutionary owner. But he also hopes to join the nobility through his son's marriage: 'il épouse une fille d'une famille ... Ah! il sera dans peu quelque chose. J'espère par son moyen arranger tout' (*OC*, 64; *Éc*, 245). And here, finally, Courier suggests to Cadet that his aims are incompatible: 'vous voudriez par son moyen voir la haute société et ne point restituer. – Justement. – Garder l'hôtel de *chose* et y recevoir le marquis ? – C'est cela. – Vous aurez de la peine'.

Because Courier's irony is pervasive, some may wonder whether, overall, it embodies something embedded in his general view of the world.

---

woodlands, Andrée Corvol-Dessert, 'Bois, Forêts', in Dictionnaire *de l'Ancien Régime*, 164–5.

11 'Cadet Rousselle a trois maisons, / Qui n'ont ni poutres, ni chevrons, [...] C'est pour loger les hirondelles' (*Cadet Rousselle* (1792)).

We owe one such interpretation to Crouzet, for whom irony arises from the senselessness of the world as Courier saw it. His writing is a

> synthèse de la révolte politique [...] et d'un nihilisme radical [...] le pamphlet dénonce le règne du non-sens ou du sens à l'envers. La Restauration n'est lisible et dicible, qu'à travers des schémas d'inversion, comme un monde sens dessus dessous. (*Éc* Préface, 36)

Here 'nihilisme radical' presumably means extreme scepticism about the existence or the application of moral values. Clearly, Courier recounts many events that are unjust or bizarre, as Crouzet's references confirm. Regarding the role of irony in conveying this picture,

> Courier produit un effet d'égarement et de confusion: il fait parler l'absurdité, adopte son discours, lui donne raison, et dans un tel brouillage que le lecteur marque un temps d'hésitation; le double langage d'une ironie généralisée est pratiquement l'essentiel de l'argumentaire du pamphlet. (*Éc* Préface, 37)

There are indeed ironic passages which can slide into obscurity for the reader, but do they fully justify Crouzet's interpretation? No doubt Courier 'dénonce le règne du non-sens', but he seems to keep his own bearings and to be able to generally articulate and decry the absurdities around him. An example is a case cited by Crouzet himself, from the *Pétition aux deux Chambres*, 'un procès pour bonapartisme où les seuls serviteurs de Bonaparte sont les juges qui condamnent les prévenus' (*Éc* Préface, p. 36). Under the Restoration, ex-Bonapartists could indeed try others for Bonapartism (*OC*, 6–7; *Éc*, 127). But the judges' political inconsistency is clear, and Courier states it plainly, without the giddying 'ironie généralisée' invoked by Crouzet. This is of course only one example, and it is not suggested that Michel Crouzet is radically wrong, but that his interpretation is overstated.

Personally, I prefer to say that irony is a polemical weapon, whose great virtue is that it enables Courier to confound his opponents with attitudes that are their own or can plausibly be attributed to them. Importantly, his irony helps create a sense that the writer remains detached from the situations that he describes. The most obvious cases are those in which personae are used, as we have just seen. At times, too, authorial detachment is suggested by the quiet tone of ironic understatement, as in the dialogue with Cadet Roussel, or when, reporting that Mauclair is imprisoned for speaking ill or badly of the government, the text comments that it was 'un peu sévère' (*Chambres*, *OC*, 4; *Éc*, 125). In Courier's political pamphlets, irony is not usually angry or sarcastic, as it may well be in some polemicists such as Chateaubriand.[12]

12 See Michel Lelièvre, *Chateaubriand polémiste* (Paris: Presses Universitaires de France, 1983), e.g. 41–2, 73. To be complete, however, it is worth noting two pamphlets the *Lettre à M. Renouard* and the *Lettre à MM. de l'Académie des Inscriptions et Belle-Lettres*. These are not examined in this study because they are not primarily political, but designed rather to defend Courier's reputation as a scholar. These pieces are highly adversarial, and show clearly that Courier was well armed with teeth and claws, but did not generally choose to use them.

Epilogue

As of his letters from Italy, Courier demonstrated impartiality and considerable breadth of outlook, most notably in understanding insurgents and occupied populations. His objectivity did not of course prevent him from being an incisive critic of activities and values that were thoroughly accepted at the time, particularly wars of conquest and the pursuit of military glory. This aspect of his outlook was all the more remarkable because his scepticism dates from a period when Napoleon's power was nearing its zenith.

In his political pamphlets, Courier writes consistently in defence of the humble, sometimes individuals as in the *Pétition aux deux Chambres*, sometimes categories, as in his general defence of smallholders. Individual freedom is his main priority, followed closely by the security and the material needs of the working poor. In the latter respects, the pamphlets uphold advances stemming from the Revolution, and may in that respect be regarded as conservative. A further conservative trait is the stress on the practical importance of morality. Courier's view of human nature is, in general, pessimistic, and he does not subscribe to the major liberal theme of the perfectibility of humanity, even if 'perfectibility' refers to a mere possibility of moral progress. What he does emphasize is that morality is independent of religion; others may have shared this view, but it remained rather unusual. At all events, he clearly conveyed that the moral impact of the Catholic clergy on the laity was generally intrusive rather than constructive.

Regarding institutional structures, he expresses general scepticism and, logically enough, has no marked preferences between forms of government. The pamphlets are not revolutionary: they do not, for example, seek to overthrow the monarchy or the Bourbons. But he is certainly critical of the authorities, especially of authority figures with a role in everyday rural life: mayors, prefects, priests, prosecutors, and gendarmes. The one institution that he criticizes as such is probably the Church, both for the constraints which it imposed on its clergy and for its intrusions into the lives of the laity. With that exception, when he criticizes an institution, he highlights human failings more than organization and rules: the mentality of the judges, for example, concerns him more than the formal procedures of the courts. In short, Courier is as much a moralist as a political thinker.

Apart from his excessively sweeping condemnations of the aristocracy, his strictures seem to be soundly based on reality. Though he shares various liberal themes, his concern and familiarity with the struggles of the rural *peuple* radically differentiate his writings from those of notable liberal thinkers such as Constant. Though there are parallels, Courier is not simply another liberal writer, or another popularizer of liberal ideas, as Bertier seems to suggest, he is *sui generis*. He is indeed a persistently independent, dissident author, willing to assail any doctrine or current of opinion.

As for his characteristics as a controversialist, we have seen his pamphlets take on various forms. Though the *Pétition* was submitted in writing, it has some features of the speech. The early *Lettres* are brief and tightly focused but, from *Lettre V* onwards, the pamphlets take a variety of forms: narrative, oration, dialogue, or extended miscellany. Though not always equally felicitous, of course, these various manners are usually successful. The unifying factor in all of this is his ability to find a style that seems appropriate to the speaker (who may be a persona), to the genre and to the subject. If one word summed up his manner, it would be 'decorum'. And though, in general, his manner seems to cohere with the matter in hand, the range is such as to suggest also unending experimentation. From this point of view, I venture a speculation: Courier's texts convey real concern with substance, but also some degree of detachment; and his relative detachment, his freedom from excessive vehemence, may arise from counterbalancing concern, as a writer, to write well in each new style which he essays.

In our world, where government is at best by imperfect democracy, restrictive 'emergency' legislation or pervasive surveillance, and where public opinion is buffeted by doctrines new and old aggressively propagated in simplistic clichés, Courier will still speak to us, if we are willing to listen.

Bibliography

Archives

Censeur Européen, <https://gallica.bnf.fr/ark:/12148/cb32738488r/>, date accessed on 22 March 2024.

Gazette Nationale ou Moniteur Universel, <https://gallica.bnf.fr/ark:/12148/cb34452336z/>, date accessed on 22 March 2024.

Texts

Calvin, Jean, *Institution de la religion chrestienne*, ed. Jacques Pannier, 4 vols (Paris: Les Belles Lettres, 1961).

Carnot, J.-F., *Examen des lois des 17, 26 mai, 9 juin 1819, et 31 mars 1820* (Paris: Nève, 1820).

Chateaubriand, François-René de, *Génie du christianisme*, 4 vols (Paris: Migneret, 1803).

Chateaubriand, François-René de, *De la Monarchie selon la Charte* (Paris : Le Normant, 1816).

Commynes, Philippe de, *Mémoires* in *Historiens et chroniqueurs du moyen âge*, ed. Albert Pauphilet and Edmond Pognon (Paris: Gallimard (Pléiade), 1952).

Constant, Benjamin, *Écrits politiques*, ed. Marcel Gauchet (Paris : Gallimard (Folio), 1997).

Constant, Benjamin, *Œuvres*, ed. Alfred Roulin (Paris : Gallimard (Pléiade), 1957).

Courier, Paul-Louis, *Correspondance générale*, ed. Geneviève Viollet-le-Duc, 3 vols (Paris: Klincksieck, vol. I (1787–1807), 1976. Paris: Klincksieck, vol. II (1808–14), 1978. Paris: Nizet, vol. III (1815–25), 1986).

Courier, Paul-Louis, *Œuvres complètes*, ed. Maurice Allem (Paris: Gallimard (Pléiade), 1951).

Courier, Paul-Louis, *Une Écriture du défi*, ed. Michel Crouzet (Paris: Kimé, 2007).

Destutt de Tracy, Antoine, *Quels sont les moyens de fonder la morale chez un peuple?* (Paris: Agasse, an VI, 1797–8).

Isocrates, *Encomium of Helen*, Isocrates, vol. III (Cambridge, MA: Harvard U. P. (Loeb Classical Library), 1945).

Isocrates, *Nicocles*, Isocrates, vol. I (Cambridge, MA: Harvard U. P. (Loeb Classical Library), 1928).

La Bruyère, Jean de, *Les Caractères*, ed. Robert Pignarre (Paris: Garnier-Flammarion, 1965).

Laërtius, Diogenes, *Lives and Opinions of Eminent Philosophers* (Cambridge, MA: Harvard U. P. (Loeb Classical Library), 1925).

Rabelais, François, *Œuvres complètes*, ed. Mireille Huchon (Paris: Gallimard (Pléiade), 1994).

Rials, Stéphane (ed.), *Textes constitutionnels français*, 17th edn (Paris: Presses Universitaires de France (Que sais-je?), 2002).

Staël, Germaine de, *De la littérature considérée dans ses rapports avec les institutions sociales*, 2 vols (Paris: Maradan, 1799).

Secondary Works

Auerbach, Erich, 'Paul-Louis Courier', *Deutsche Vierteljahrsschrift für Literaturwissenschaft und Geistesgeschichte*, 4 (1926), 514–47.

Bertier de Sauvigny, G. de, *La Restauration* (Paris: Flammarion, 1955).

Cadet, Nicolas, 'Anatomie d'une "petite guerre", la campagne de Calabre de 1806–1807', *Revue d'histoire du XIX*[e] *siècle*, 30 (2005), on line.

Cobban, Alfred, *History of Modern France*, 3 vols (Harmondsworth: Penguin Books, 1961–5).

Collins, Irene, *Liberalism in Nineteenth-Century Europe* (London: The Historical Association, 1957).

Damamme, Jean-Claude, *Les Soldats de la Grande Armée* (Paris: Perrin, 1998).

Dejammet, Alain, *Paul-Louis Courier* (Paris: Fayard, 2009).

Duggan, Christopher, *The Force of Destiny: A History of Italy since 1796* (London: Penguin Books, 2008).

Dwyer, Philip, *Napoleon: The Path to Power 1769–1799* (London: Bloomsbury, 2007).

Dwyer, Philip, *Citizen Emperor: Napoleon in Power, 1799–1815* (London: Bloomsbury, 2013).

Gaschet, Robert, *Paul-Louis Courier et la Restauration* (Paris: Hachette, 1913).

Huchon, Mireille, 'Courier lecteur de Rabelais', *Cahiers Paul-Louis Courier*, 2/4 (1980), 7–13.

Lautman, Jean-Pierre, *Paul-Louis Courier, ou la plume indomptée* (Chambray-lès-Tours: Éditions CLD, 2001).

Lentz, Thierry, *Joseph Bonaparte* (Paris: Perrin, 2016).
Lentz, Thierry, *Napoléon: Dictionnaire historique* (Paris: Perrin, 2020).
Petrucci, Sandro, 'Opposizione popolare, insorgenza e brigantaggio nell'Italia napoleonica', *Annali di storia moderna e contemporanea*, 14 (2008), 259–80.
Price, Munro, *The Perilous Crown* (London: Pan Macmillan, 2008).
Sainte-Beuve, Charles-Augustin, *Causeries du lundi*, 3rd edn, 15 vols (Paris: Garnier, 1858–72).
Sciascia, Leonardo, *Opere*, ed. Paolo Squillacioti, 3 vols (Milan: Adelphi Edizioni, 2012–19).
Teyssier, Arnaud, *Louis-Philippe: le dernier roi des Français* (Paris: Perrin, 2010).
Tulard, Jean, *Napoléon ou le mythe du sauveur* (Paris: Fayard (Collection Pluriel), 1987).
Tulard, Jean, *Les Français sous Napoléon* (Paris: Hachette, 1978).
Waresquiel, Emmanuel de, *Talleyrand: le prince immobile* (Paris: Fayard, 2006).
Waresquiel, Emmanuel de, *Penser la Restauration 1814–1830* (Paris: Tallandier (Texto), 2020).
Weinburg, Mark, 'The Social Analysis of Three Early Nineteenth-Century French Liberals: Say, Comte, and Dunoyer', *Journal of Libertarian Studies*, 2 (1978), 45–63.
Winock, Michel, *Les Voix de la Liberté: les écrivains engagés du XIX*[e] *siècle* (Paris: Éditions du Seuil, 2001).
Yvert, Benoît, 'Aux origines de l'Orléanisme. Les doctrinaires, *Le Globe* et les Bourbons', in *Guizot, les Doctrinaires et la presse* (Val Richer: Fondation Guizot, 1994), 11–33.

Reference Works

Bély, Lucien (ed.), *Dictionnaire de l'Ancien Régime* (Paris: Presses Universitaires de France, 1996).
Gougenheim, Georges, *Grammaire de la langue française du seizième siècle* (Lyons: Édition IAC, 1951).
Grevisse, Maurice, *Le Bon Usage*, 11th edn (Gembloux: Duculot, 1980).
Rey-Debove, Josette and Rey, Alain (eds), *Le Nouveau Petit Robert* (Paris: Dictionnaires Le Robert, 1993).
Trésor de la langue Française informatisé.

Index

Medieval and Early Modern French Studies

Series Editor
Noël Peacock

Striking and stimulating contributions continue to be made to French studies and cultural studies of the medieval and early modern periods. This series aims to publish work of the highest quality in these areas. The series will include monographs and collaborative or collected works from both established and younger scholars, and will encompass a wide range of disciplines and theoretical approaches. Contributions will be welcomed in French or English.

Published Volumes

Ian R. Morrison:
Paul-Louis Courier (1772–1825):
Dissident Author under Louis XVIII
2024. 154 pages. ISBN 978-1-80374-523-7

Charles Stone:
The Theatre of Martyrdom:
Performing Piety in 1640s France
2023. 140 pages. ISBN 978-1-80079-733-8

John Sayer:
Jean Racine, Echoes across Europe
2021. 266 pages. ISBN 978-1-80079-092-6

Sarah Alyn Stacey and Joanna Poetz (eds):
New Perspectives on Heretical Discourse and Identities: The Waldensians in Historical Context.
2021. 344 pages. ISBN 978-1-78997-714-1

Kelly Fender McConnell and Michael Meere (eds):
Coups de maître: Studies in Medieval and Early Modern Literature and Culture, in Honour of John D. Lyons.
2021. 592 pages. ISBN 978-1-78997-145-3

William Brooks:
François Boscheron, ami de Challe, ses œuvres, ses biographies et ses travaux éditoriaux: Une enquête bio-bibliographique.
2020. 472 pages. ISBN 978-1-78997-408-9

Catherine Emerson (ed.):
'Le Bel Épy qui foisonne'. Collection and Translation in French Print Networks, 1476–1576.
2019. 146 pages. ISBN 978-1-78707-773-77

Richard Maber and Joanna Barker (eds):
Managing Time. Literature and Devotion in Early Modern France.
2017. 278 pages. ISBN 978-1-78707-492-7

Sarah Alyn Stacey (ed.):
Political, Religious and Social Conflict in the States of Savoy, 1400–1700.
2014. 331 pages. ISBN 978-3-0343-0831-1

Susanna Phillippo:
Hellenic Whispers. Modes of Greek Literary Influence in Seventeenth-Century French Drama.
2013. 593 pages. ISBN 978-3-0343-0851-9

Walter E. Rex:
Molière's Strategies. Timely Reflections on his Art of Comedy.
2013. 350 pages. ISBN 978-3-0343-0920-2

William Brooks, Christine McCall Probes et Rainer Zaiser (éds):
Lieux de culture dans la France du XVIIe siècle.
2012. 315 pages. ISBN 978-3-0343-0813-7

Nicholas Hammond and Michael Moriarty (eds):
Evocations of Eloquence. Rhetoric, Literature and Religion in Early Modern France. Essays in Honour of Peter Bayley.
2012. 372 pages. ISBN 978-3-0343-0849-6

Nicholas Hammond:

Gossip, Sexuality and Scandal in France (1610–1715).
2011. 168 pages. ISBN 978-3-0343-0706-2

Jan Clarke, Pierre Pasquier et Henry Phillips (éds):

La Ville en scène en France et en Europe (1552–1709).
2011. 245 pages. ISBN 978-3-0343-0105-3

Jane Southwood and Bernard Bourque (eds):

French Seventeenth-Century Literature. Influences and Transformations. Essays in Honour of Christopher J. Gossip.
2009. 295 pages. ISBN 978-3-03911-537-2

William Brooks:

Philippe Quinault, Dramatist.
2009. 512 pages. ISBN 978-3-03911-533-4

James R. Simpson:

Troubling Arthurian Histories. Court Culture, Performance and Scandal in Chrétien de Troyes's *Erec et Enide*.
2007. 520 pages. ISBN 978-3-03911-385-9

Adriana Bontea:

Les Origines de la comédie française classique.
2007. 284 pages. ISBN 978-3-03911-123-7

William Brooks and Rainer Zaiser (eds):

Religion, Ethics, and History in the French Long Seventeenth Century / La Religion, la morale, et l'histoire à l'âge classique.
2007. 348 pages. ISBN 978-3-03911-104-6

William Brooks and Rainer Zaiser (eds):

Theatre, Fiction, and Poetry in the French Long Seventeenth Century / Le Théâtre, le roman, et la poésie à l'âge classique.
2007. 322 pages. ISBN 978-3-03911-103-9